B

Rhythm, Relationships, and Transcendence

Rhythm, Relationships, and Transcendence

✦

Patterns in the Complex Web of Life

Toru Sato Ph.D.
Illustration on cover by Yoshiko Sato

Writers Club Press
New York Lincoln Shanghai

Rhythm, Relationships, and Transcendence
Patterns in the Complex Web of Life

Writers Club Press
an imprint of iUniverse, Inc.

For information address:
iUniverse
2021 Pine Lake Road, Suite 100
Lincoln, NE 68512
www.iuniverse.com

ISBN: 0-595-26222-8

Printed in the United States of America

Dear Readers,

This book is dedicated to Yoshiko, my teacher, and partner of life

"We are all one child, spinning through Mother Sky" (Shawnee Native Tribe)

Contents

List of Illustrations

Preface

Growing up, listening, reading, and experiencing many things throughout my life, I was exposed to many theories, ideas, and stories to help me understand my everyday existence. Most of these theories were extremely insightful and have been instrumental in developing my understanding of things. As wonderful as they were, these ideas and theories were either only applicable to a limited set of experiences or extremely complex and beyond my comprehension abilities. This dissatisfaction has driven me to search, integrate, and create a simple theory to explain as much of our experiences as possible. Due to this wonderful opportunity to learn these theories and ideas as well as experience this dissatisfaction, I feel I have been somewhat successful in this endeavor for a relatively simple theory.

It has been my dream for many years to write a book to share these discoveries I have made along my journey. In the beginning, I felt that I did not have enough insight and experience to share and when I felt I had enough to share later on, the every day things in life kept me busy enough to procrastinate and only think about writing or think about the reasons why I cannot write instead of just doing it. I have finally gathered up my courage to sit down and actually do what I have been intending to do.

In this book, I will to try to share my simple understanding of both the beautiful and sometimes seemingly horrifying things that occur in life in hopes that it may help some of us understand similar types of experiences that we have in our lives. As you read this, please keep in mind that this is only one way to understand our experiences among many. It is not the right way or a better way. There is a proverb by the Blackfoot native tribe in North America that translates, "There are many paths to a meaningful sense of the natural world." Thus, I suggest these ideas put forth in this book not as dogma, but as a possible path and a theory in progress.

While we are looking at the big picture, I would also like to mention that, like any organism, my understanding of things is in continual progress. Although I hope that my understanding will develop beyond what it is now, I would like to introduce my present understanding of things at this point in my life. Therefore, my views may change in the future as I expose myself to new and more wonderful experiences and ideas.

I have tried to structure this book so that one section leads naturally into the next section. Some of these sections assume that the reader understands what has been discussed in the previous sections. By adding bits and pieces to the understanding already established from the previous sections, I am hoping that many readers enjoy progressing through the book smoothly. Due to this structure, however, some readers may find some parts of this book overly simplistic and others may find other parts of the book overly theoretical. Furthermore, many readers may also find various parts of this book to overlap in content since all of the ideas discussed in the book relate to each other in many ways. To some extent, the overlap is useful to illustrate the relationships among the various ideas and to discuss certain things from a variety of vantage points. However I understand that those readers who are well versed on this topic may find certain parts of the book repetitive for this reason. I apologize for this inconvenience since I have yet to figure out a way around this problem while still conveying my message to a wide range of readers.

Lastly I would like to mention that what I am about to explain is not completely new and original. The ideas discussed in this book may most adequately be considered as a unique interpretation and integration of what many other individuals have mentioned in many different ways. Thus, I am extremely grateful for the many individuals who have contributed to my understanding of what is written in this book. Some of these individuals are well-known writers/scholars whose works I am only beginning to understand and others are family members and friends who have shared important insights through their everyday behaviors and attitudes as well as the conversations I have had with them. These individuals are not limited to, but include (in alphabetical order) Robert Abelson, Hugh Aberman, Connie Adkins, Alfred Adler, Andras Angyal, James H. Austin, Richard Bach, David Bakan, Martin S. Banks, Doug Benson, Aaron T. Beck, Eric Berne, Sidney Blatt, David Bohm, Niels Bohr, George Boeree, Medard Boss, Jim Cameron, Fritjof Capra, Richard Carlson, Robert C. Carson, Angela Caudill, Nancy Chodorow, Bradley Clough, Arthur Combs, Mihalyi Csikszentmihalyi, Dale Dickson, Larry Dossey, John Dovidio, Albert Einstein, Albert Ellis, Erik Erikson, Ronald Fairbairn, Leon Festinger, Richard Feynman, Viktor Fränkl, Anna Freud, Sigmund Freud, Erich Fromm, Timothy Gallway, Samuel Gaertner, Carol Gilligan, James Gleick, Irving Goffman, Daniel Goleman, John Gottman, Brian Greene, Leslie Greenberg, Alex Grey, Vittorio Guidano, Harry Guntrip, Rachel Harris, Stephen Hawking, Werner Heisenberg, Tory Higgins, Karen Horney, Aldous Huxley, William James, Irving Janis, Erich Jantsch, Julian Jaynes, Spencer Johnson, Carl Jung, Michio Kaku, Anne Katherine, Keiko Kato, Kengo Kato, Mikiko Kato, Otto Kernberg, Donald Kiesler, Shinobu Kitayama, Melanie Klein, Arthur Koestler, Lawrence Kohlberg, Heinz Kohut, Jiddu Krishnamurti, Elizabeth Kübler-Ross, Thomas Kuhn, Kenichi Kushido, Timothy Leary, Daniel Levinson, Kurt Lewin, Jim Loehr, James Lovelock, Lester Luborsky, Jeffrey Mann, Lynn Margulis, Hazel R. Markus, Abraham Maslow, Bruce Mattingly, Umberto Maturana, Rollo May, Doug McCann, Phillip McGraw, Pia Mellody, Jean Baker Miller, Salvatore Minuchin, Takeshi Miyamoto, Stephen Mitchell, Caroline Myss, Audrey Murrell, Dorothy Law Nolte, Shinya Nishina, I. P. Pavlov, Robert Peck, Candace Pert, Jean Piaget, Robert Pirsig, Ilya Prigogine, Otto Rank, James Redfield, William Reich, David Reiss, Carl Rogers, Carl Sagan, Naganobu Sato, Sanae Sato, Yoshiko Sato, Crispin Sartwell, Joyce Saunders, Stanley Schachter, Roger Shank, Rupert

Sheldrake, Muzafer Sherif, Jerome Singer, B. F. Skinner, Donald Snygg, Daniel Stern, Hans Strupp, Harry Stack Sullivan, Stella Ting-Toomey, Adrian Tomer, Hiroyuki Uesaka, Setsu Uesaka, Francisco Varela, Roger Walsh, Katja Walters, Alan Watts, Paul Watzlawick, John Weakland, Ken Wilber, Stephen Wolinsky, Jerry Wiggins, D. W. Winnicott, Charles Whitfield, Ju Yamada, Gary Zukav as well as various religions, philosophies, and traditions of people in many cultures around the world. Finally, I would also like to thank Yoshiko Sato in helping me create the figures in this book. I am most certain that I have left some important people out. My greatest apologies to anyone I have fool-hardily left out.

Having mentioned all of this, let's get it on!

Rhythm in Relationships: Rhythm of our Psyche

GIVING AND RECEIVING

The Mohawk native tribe in North America has a proverb that translates, "Life is both giving and receiving". All of us have heard of this type of expression in some form or another in our lives. Most of us relate this to interpersonal relationships. When people talk about relationships they say you have to give and receive (or take). I'll clean our bathroom if you do our laundry. I'll go to your favorite store with you if you go to my favorite restaurant with me afterwards. I'll give and then I'll receive (or take). In a nastier context, we have the expression "getting even with someone". When someone takes something from you, you take something back from him or her. Again, you are giving and then taking, although perhaps not as gracefully in this case.

This is all common sense to us regardless of what culture you are from. The question is, "What are we giving and receiving?" In some cases it is clear. I go to the store and I pay the store clerk a dollar and the store clerk gives me a candy bar. I get a candy bar and s/he gets a dollar. We both gave and received and the interaction went smoothly. In this case, we are actually trading material goods and therefore we can actually *see* what we gave and received. In other cases, it is more difficult to see what we give and receive. Let's take an example mentioned earlier, "I'll go to your favorite store if you go to my favorite restaurant with me afterwards." In this case, two people are doing certain things that may be considered as giving and receiving but they are not trading any material goods. What are they giving and receiving from each

1

other here? The other example mentioned earlier was, "I'll clean our bathroom if you do our laundry." Again, the two people involved are not trading any material goods but we still consider this giving and receiving. Why are all of these examples of giving and receiving? What is it that we are giving and receiving?

Let's think about this for a while. We feel we are giving when we feel like we are doing something for someone or something else rather than for ourselves and we feel like we are receiving if something is being done for ourselves rather than for other people or things. If we give too much without receiving, we feel tired, depleted, controlled, used, abused, or just plain bad. If we receive much without giving, we feel important, respected, attractive, in control, attended to, accepted, cared for, energized, or just plain good. And to keep a relationship working, both sides need to feel important, respected, attractive, in control, attended to, accepted, cared for, energized, or just plain good to a certain extent and thus we need to take turns giving and receiving. But what is this "thing" that we are giving and receiving?

ATTENTION AS ENERGY

One of the seven principles in the teachings of the Huna (wisdom from Hawaiian Shamanism) is translated as, "Energy flows where attention goes". "Attention" may be the closest English word for this "thing". Attention is the basis for acceptance, respect, influence and care, all of which we crave for in our everyday lives. Being accepted enables you to receive attention from others. Being respected enables you to receive attention from others. When people allow you to influence them, they pay attention to you. When people care about you, they give you attention. When someone does the laundry for you, you feel your desires are attended to, you are cared for, you are respected and you are accepted. When someone goes to your favorite restaurant with you, you feel that your desires are attended to, you are cared for, respected, and accepted.

When you go to your friend's favorite store with him or her even if you are not interested in the store, you are attending to, you are caring for, you are respecting, and you are accepting the desires[1] of your friend.

Throughout history, people have discussed concepts similar to this "thing" in the past and called it "psychic energy", or used the Chinese term "Chi", the Indian term "Prana", or the Japanese term "Ki", or the term "Ka" in Egyptian lore among many others. For the sake of simplicity, let us simply call this thing "energy". We call this "energy" because we feel energized when others pay attention to us. We also call this "energy" because we feel depleted of energy when others do not pay attention to us, do not respect our desires, do not care for us, do not accept us for who we are.

What is interesting about this is that all relationships have this characteristic of repeating this process of giving and receiving. We live in a rhythmic cycle of giving and receiving in all of our relationships, whether it is your relationship with your spouse, child, parent, business partner, client, coworker, friend, neighbor etc. Figure 1 is an example of this. Let's consider this conversation between two friends, Priscilla and Joanne.

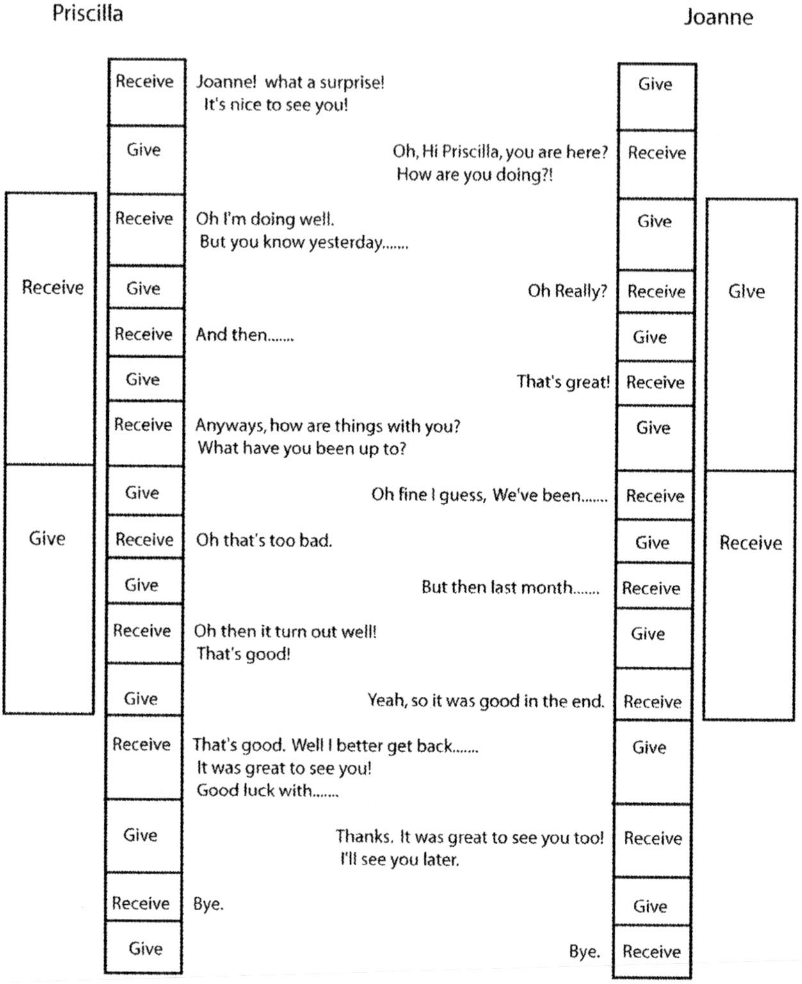

Priscilla   Joanne

	Receive	Joanne! what a surprise! It's nice to see you!	Give
	Give	Oh, Hi Priscilla, you are here? How are you doing?!	Receive
Receive	Receive	Oh I'm doing well. But you know yesterday.......	Give	Give
	Give	Oh Really?	Receive
	Receive	And then.......	Give
	Give	That's great!	Receive
	Receive	Anyways, how are things with you? What have you been up to?	Give
Give	Give	Oh fine I guess, We've been.......	Receive	Receive
	Receive	Oh that's too bad.	Give
	Give	But then last month.......	Receive
	Receive	Oh then it turn out well! That's good!	Give
	Give	Yeah, so it was good in the end.	Receive
	Receive	That's good. Well I better get back....... It was great to see you! Good luck with.......	Give
	Give	Thanks. It was great to see you too! I'll see you later.	Receive
	Receive	Bye.	Give
	Give	Bye.	Receive

Figure 1. Giving and Taking in Conversation

In the conversation in Figure 1 we have two people taking turns giving and receiving energy or attention and respect. First, Priscilla speaks and Joanne pays attention and shows respect for Priscilla. Then Joanne speaks and Priscilla pays attention and shows respect for Joanne. And then, Priscilla speaks and Joanne pays attention and shows respect for

Priscilla. This goes on and on until the conversation loses its momentum and eventually ends.

If we take a closer look, we notice that in the first half of the conversation, Priscilla speaks about what is going on in her life for a while as Joanne provides only small bits of the conversation (e.g., Oh really & That's great!) to maintain the rhythm and to show that she is absorbing what Joanne is saying. Afterwards the roles are reversed. In the second half of the conversation Joanne speaks about what is going on in her life for a while as Priscilla provides only small bits of the conversation (e.g., Oh that's too bad & Oh then it turned out well! That's good!) just to maintain the rhythm and to show that she is absorbing what Joanne is saying. In this way, Joanne gives and Priscilla receives energy in the first half and then Priscilla gives and Joanne receives energy in the second half of the conversation. Notice that within the larger general rhythm (see outer labels), there is also a smaller finer rhythm in this conversation (see inner labels). Most relationships including our own function in a rhythmic fashion of giving and receiving energy and there are rhythms within rhythms within rhythms if we look very closely. Usually, the more you give, the more you receive and the more you receive, the more you give. This implies that we can take varying amounts of energy from each other. Let's examine what things influence the amount of energy we give or receive.

ENERGY EXCHANGE AND MOTIVATION

We can give and take energy in varying degrees. If you graciously ask someone to stop smoking in your house, you are asking him or her to attend to and respect your desires a little bit. In other words, you may be taking a little bit of energy. The other person being asked to stop smoking may feel that they have given a bit of energy. If you yell and physically assault someone in order to make him or her stop smoking in your house you are taking massive amounts of energy in a short amount of time. In the same way, the other person being yelled at and assaulted may feel that he or she has lost or given away massive amounts of energy.

We can also take massive amounts of energy if we take little by little for a prolonged period of time without giving back. This is why we feel exhausted if someone talks to us incessantly for a long time without letting you have your turn. This incessantly speaking person is not yelling at us or physically assaulting us but we feel tired and very low in energy after a while. In this case, the person is taking energy little by little but doing so incessantly for a long period of time without giving much back to you. After a while, this adds up and you end up losing a lot of energy! This usually does not work well in a relationship because there is no rhythm of giving and taking. There is just taking (or just giving if you look at it from the other person's perspective).

In general the more energy we lose, the worse we feel. The more energy we gain, receive, or take, the better we feel. This is the ugly part of this theory. In a sense we live in a competitive world. We compete for "energy". This is why many of us want to be famous, want to do heroic things, want to be powerful and influential, want more money. These are all means to gain energy. Being a hero or being famous makes us attract a lot of attention and admiration and sometimes respect. In other words, we receive energy when we're famous. Moreover, having social power is nothing more that being in a position where you can receive more energy than you are obligated to give. Social power, whether it comes from being a bully in school or the president of a company, makes other people attend to you more than you attend to them. The person with less social power usually attends to what the powerful person wants and tries to respond to him or her appropriately all of the time. The person with more social power is much less obligated to attend to what other less powerful people desire. Money is also just another symbol for "energy". People who have more money attract a lot of attention from others because others want their money or what their money can afford. People with lots of money can afford better service (which is defined basically as more attention), and can buy products that energize them easily (such as high-quality food, beautiful cars and houses, vacations, etc.). All of this seems a bit ugly but if you hang in there and read further, you will find that there are also many more beautiful things in life for all of us. But before we go into that, let's go back to relationships for now.

RELATIONSHIP TEXTURES

Different relationships have different textures. Some of them are very stable and function gracefully and others are less stable and are action packed. For example, Gwen and Stephen have a relationship where both individuals are very tender, attentive, and sensitive to each other, giving and receiving relatively equal amounts of energy from each other. This type of relationship can be represented by diagram 3 in Figure 2. The vertical lines in the figure represent the amount of energy each individual is receiving. The horizontal axis represents time. In this case, although one of the two individuals is giving slightly more than the other at any given moment (and thus we perceive this as giving and taking), both Gwen and Stephen are giving and receiving relatively similar amounts of energy at every moment. Individuals in this kind of relationship are generally seen as relatively attentive, sensitive and tender and the relationship is seen as relatively stable. As we can sense from the image of Diagram 3 in Figure 2, Gwen and Stephen have what many of us would call a smooth relationship.

Person A

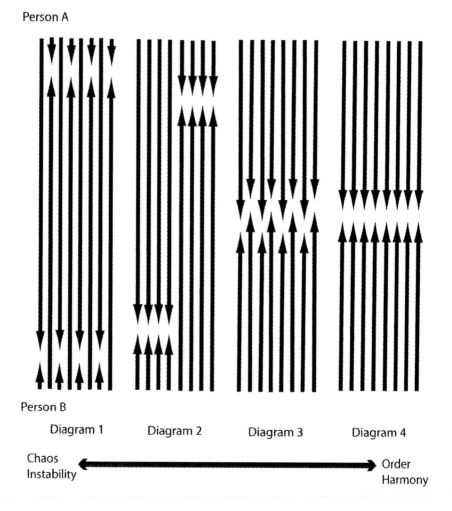

Person B

Diagram 1   Diagram 2   Diagram 3   Diagram 4

Chaos   Order
Instability ◄──────────────────────────────► Harmony

Figure 2. Relationship Textures

Other people can have a relationship where both individuals are very insensitive and aggressive toward each other, giving and taking massive amounts of energy from each other. For example, Anthony and Beth are very insensitive and aggressive toward each other. This type of interaction is illustrated in Diagram 2 Figure 2. In this case, Anthony gives very little energy and receives a high amount of energy in the beginning and then, Beth gives very little energy and receives a high amount of energy afterwards. Individuals in this kind of relationship are generally seen as relatively insensitive and aggressive and the relationship is seen as relatively unstable. This is often witnessed in stories of revenge. Anthony is disrespectful to Beth and so the Beth does something disrespectful to Anthony. As the image of Diagram 2 in Figure 2 suggests, it's what many of us call a rocky relationship. If the conflict escalates, we sometimes end up having an even more chaotic situation where two individuals are almost simultaneously yelling at each other without really listening to each other (even though they are both affected by the other person yelling). This type of interaction can be illustrated as the image of Diagram 1 in Figure 2. All of these types of relationships work as long as they are giving and receiving (or taking) equal amounts of energy from each other. Sometimes, the same two people can be very sensitive and tender to each other on one day and then be very insensitive and aggressive to each other on another day. We all have good days and bad days. As long as there is a rhythm of giving and receiving with equal amounts of energy going back and forth between two individuals, the relationship can be maintained.

If, on the other hand, the individuals involved do not give and receive equal amounts of energy, the relationship has a lower chance of surviving. Nobody wants to constantly give without receiving attention, acceptance, and respect (energy). If you have become involved in a relationship like this, you are most likely going to leave and abandon that relationship. If you don't leave the relationship, it does not necessarily mean that you are a very giving person (although this may happen in very rare cases). In most cases, it means that you are gaining something, some energy, by staying in the relationship but you are not consciously aware of what you are gaining.

Let's consider a relationship with an abusive husband and an abused wife. By abusing his wife, the husband is essentially forcing her to attend to him and respect him without attending to her desires or respecting her. Thus, the husband is constantly gaining energy by abusing his wife. There is no reason for the husband to leave. The wife is constantly losing energy to her abusive husband. Why is she still in the relationship? There may be numerous possibilities. She may gain financial security (i.e., energy) by staying with her husband. She may be constantly gaining energy by receiving pity from her neighbors. She may feel protected by her husband from outsiders who she considers to be even more harmful. She may be afraid to leave because her husband threatens to kill her if she does and thus avoids potential death, which is considered to be an extreme loss of energy. She may be afraid of losing respect and acceptance (i.e., energy) from her relatives for leaving her husband. Usually, it is a combination of various reasons but in one way or another the abused person has something to gain by staying in the relationship. The person either is able to gain energy from others (sometimes from an outside source) or is able to protect him or herself from losing energy by staying in the relationship.

NAME OF THE GAME

Many of us think that they would rather have a smooth relationship rather than a rocky relationship because rocky relationships increase stress in our lives. Many of us would rather have a more relaxing life than the hectic lives they have. Of course, a lot of the hectic stuff comes from rocky relationships. Much of our stress in our everyday lives come from the rockiness of our relationships. We end up competing for energy and sometimes even literally kill each other in the process (indirectly by causing each other excessive stress).

So the question is "How can we have a smoother relationship with others?" We often hear the expression, "What goes around, comes around." Although we must be careful not to oversimplify and overgeneralize this statement, in many cases, what you give is what you get or what you take is what is taken from you afterwards. If you are aggressive and take large amounts of energy from your spouse, chances are that your spouse will do the same back to you to replenish his or her energy that he or she lost to you. If you are tender and caring and take only minimal amounts of energy from your spouse, chances are that your spouse will be tender and caring toward you as well because he or she does not lose much energy and therefore does not feel the desire to replenish much energy. We will find out later that the whole picture is more complicated than that because every relationship exists within other relationships but overall, this is the gist of the story.

Figure 3 is a diagram displaying different experiences that we as individuals have with particular other individuals at any given moment. Any experience can be placed somewhere in this two dimensional space. The right end of the horizontal dimension represents unity or a sense of togetherness and the left end represents separation or a sense of detachment. Top end of the vertical dimension represents dominance, influence or a sense of control. One's level on this side of the dimension represents how much energy you are receiving. The more dominant, controlling and influential we are, the more energy we receive. The bottom end of the vertical dimension represents submission, absorption or a sense of being influenced or controlled. One's level on this side of the dimension represents how much energy you are giving away. The more submissive we are, the more we are influenced or controlled by others, the more energy we give away.

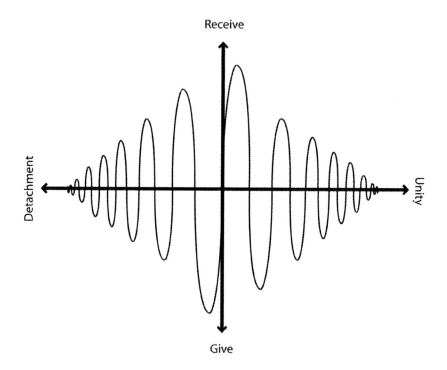

Figure 3. Spectrum of Relationship Experiences

The waves represent the rhythmic nature of our experiences of giving and receiving. They also provide a general indication of the emotional stability experienced at each point on the horizontal dimension. The wavy line corresponds to the meeting point of the tips of the two arrows in Figure 2. The smaller the waves, the more emotionally stable. The more togetherness and unity one experiences with the other person, the more emotionally stable one feels. The small waves correspond to the smooth relationship illustrated earlier. The more dominant or submissive one feels toward the other person the more emotionally unstable we feel (either positively of negatively aroused) and thus the waves go up and down more radically. We feel highly dominant in one moment and then we feel highly dominated in the next moment. These large waves correspond to the experience of rocky relationships illustrated earlier. The more detached one is from someone, the less unstable we feel regarding that particular relationship. We feel less unstable because that particular relationship does not concern us at the time. It should be noted here that detachment is not a general experience in itself. We are usually detached from someone because we are focusing on a relationship with something or someone else at the time and not on the relationship in question.

Let's consider the relationship between Stephen and Gwen discussed earlier with Diagram 3 in Figure 2. In this case, both individuals are attending to each other very much and relatively equally. This is like when you are having an interaction with someone and everything is clicking. You can relate to each other extremely well and it feels great. You feel like you finally found a person who you can really understand and who can really understand you. When you are in love with someone, it is sort of like this as well. But when you are in love, there are other things going on in addition to this such as your hormones running wild throughout your body. Regardless of what the exact situation is, when this happens, both individuals feel a sense of peaceful unity or togetherness with each other. This experience for both individuals in this type of relationship is represented as a spot close to the right end of the horizontal axis of Figure 3. The waves are small, meaning both individuals experience emotional stability and feel calm and relaxed in general.

In contrast, if we go back and consider the relationship between Anthony and Beth with Diagram 2 in Figure 2, we have a different story. First you have one person dominating the relationship or taking lots of energy from the other and then you have the other person dominating the relationship or taking lots of energy from the other. The waves are large like the middle of the horizontal dimension in Figure 3. Indeed, this experience for both individuals in the relationship is represented at the middle of the horizontal axis where Anthony is highly dominating and Beth feels highly dominated (submission) and so then Beth responds by being highly dominant and making Anthony feel dominated (submission) and this cycle goes on and on. In other words, Anthony takes massive amounts of energy from Beth and then Beth takes massive amounts of energy from Anthony and then Anthony takes massive amounts of energy from Beth again and this cycle continues until at least one of them realizes the futility of what they are doing. In sum, the smoother our relationships, the more unity / togetherness we feel with what we are directly interacting with. The rougher our relationships, the less unity / togetherness we feel with what we are directly interacting with.

So as you may have guessed by now, the name of the game is, "paying close attention every moment". In order to have a smoother relationship, we need to attend to each other's desires, respect each other, accept each other, not in just every moment of the interaction but every moment of our lives (whether they are in our immediate presence or not). If you attend to the other person's desires, if you can accept and respect the other person, you will not behave too aggressively, you will not behave in an insensitive manner. You will not take large amounts of energy. And if you do not take large amounts of energy from others, others are less likely to be depleted of energy and are less likely to take large amounts of energy from you. You are more likely to have smooth relationships than rocky relationships. You can move from the middle to the right side of the horizontal axis. We move from a rough and intense wave of giving and receiving to a fine wave of giving and receiving. This is what we intuitively mean when we say, "I am doing fine" or "I am having a rough time". You may have noticed that in Figure 3, the wave is "fine" when we are having a smooth relationship with others but the wave is also "fine" when we are very detached. How does that work? Are we also fine when we are detached? Let's examine this in more detail.

SEPARATION / DETACHMENT

In Figure 3, we have examined the differences between the middle of the horizontal axis and the right side of the horizontal axis. What about the left side? I mentioned that the left end of this axis represents separation or a sense of detachment earlier. What this implies is that the left side of the horizontal axis corresponds to the relationships we have with things that we are not directly engaged with. The left side of this horizontal axis considers the fact that we are simultaneously embedded in many relationships. You may have a relationship with your son and a relationship with your spouse among many others. Let's take these two relationships as a simple example to explain the concept of separation / detachment. When you are at home and interacting with your spouse in the kitchen while your son is in his room playing his guitar to her girlfriend, you are relating to your spouse more than you are relating to your son. And thus you are on the right side of the horizontal axis in terms of your relationship with your spouse but on the left side of the horizontal axis in terms of your relationship with your son. While you are interacting with your spouse in this case, you still may be interacting with your son in a remote way. For example, you may hear his guitar playing from the kitchen and thus you are slightly attending to your son's behavior and your experience of those moments is ever so slightly influenced by your son's behavior. Your son may also hear you speaking to your spouse from his room even though he may not be paying much attention to what you are saying. In a sense, your son is slightly attending to your behavior and his experience of those moments is ever so slightly influenced by your behavior. In this case, you and your son are slightly detached from each other because both of you are attending to something other than each other more intensely. In your case this something other may be your spouse. In your son's case it may be his girlfriend to whom he is playing his guitar.

The less attention you and your son pay to each other, the less you influence each other, the more detached you are from each other and the further left you go on the horizontal axis. However, the less attention you pay to your son, the more attention you are paying to someone or something else. You only fail to attend to something when you are attending to something else. This is how attention works. You cannot pay attention to absolutely nothing just as you cannot pay attention to absolutely everything. Thus complete detachment with something means complete attention to something else. They are both the same state of mind.

When neither individual is paying any attention to the other, there is complete detachment. At this point the wave becomes just a straight line characterizing no interaction or no relationship. However, the concept of the straight line or the concept of complete detachment does not really exist on a physical level (i.e., as long as we physically exist). We are all connected to one another in some way. Although the connectedness goes beyond the physical plane, let's use the physical plane as a simple example. If I wave my hand in the air, I move the air around my hand, which moves the air around that, which moves the air around that, which will vibrate windows and walls ever so slightly, which will move the air on the other side of the wall and windows, which will move the air around that, which will eventually move all of the air in the entire atmosphere of the planet at some microscopic level. Although most relationships may be extremely indirect and remote, what you do influences everything and everyone in some way.

On the other hand, we can also say that the more active we are physically and emotionally, the more we interact with and the less detached we are from the things we are not directly engaged with. So if you were yelling loudly at your spouse, you are not only influencing your spouse. You are also influencing your son upstairs because he can hear you more than before even though you are not yelling at him. But because you are not yelling directly at your son, he is less influenced by the yelling than your spouse is. Your spouse is engaged in a deeper (more togetherness) interaction with you than your son is. Thus even though your relationship with both of those individuals at that moment are quite rocky, you are more engaged with (thus feel more togetherness with) your spouse. If we use Figure 3 to explain this example, your relationship with your spouse would be characterized as slightly to the right side of the middle of the horizontal axis and your relationship with your son would be slightly to the left side of the middle of the horizontal axis. Furthermore, if you are yelling, you would most probably be on the dominant side of the vertical axis while your spouse and son would be on the submissive side of the vertical axis.

UNITY / TOGETHERNESS

Similar to the concept of complete detachment, complete unity or complete togetherness can also be characterized as a straight line in Figure 3. Therefore, complete unity or complete togetherness is also a concept that does not really exist on the physical level. We may be able to experience something infinitely close to it, but never is it *complete* unity. Complete unity means that there is perfect harmony, perfect silence, perfect peace, or nothingness. It implies that there is no action or reaction. There is no rhythm of giving and receiving. There is no interaction. Even when we feel at one with someone, we feel united but we are not completely united. We are still in a slight rhythm of giving and receiving. This is the definition of interaction. The line has a slight wave in it even though it may look very straight from far away. We as physical beings are bundles of physical energy, and energy by definition is active and interacts with the environment. Life is continuous change and we continuously adapt to this change by interacting. Thus we cannot "not interact" as long as we physically exist. In many cultures, this concept of complete unity or perfect harmony is associated with the truth, the true self, the divine being or heaven. It is considered to be the manifestation of perfection with no glitches and no bumps. It is perhaps the state we were in before we physically existed and perhaps the state we go into after we cease to exist. Complete nothingness.

Theoretically, this complete unity / togetherness is considered to be identical to complete separation / detachment. Both states imply the absence of physical existence and thus an absence of rhythm and therefore, complete harmony. They both imply a perfectly harmonious relationship, which is the same as the absence of any relationship. In a sense, the left and right half of the horizontal axis are mirror images of each other.

The distinction is determined by our ability or perhaps our limitation to selectively attend to only a limited range of things (like specific individuals) at a time. We as human beings, with the sensory apparatus and the cognitive system that we have, cannot pay conscious attention to everything in the universe all of the time. We can only pay conscious attention to a limited amount of energy, information, or stimuli at any specific time. If am looking at point A with great intensity, I cannot look at point B twenty yards away in another direction with the same amount of intensity at the same time. Therefore, some things are attended to more than others at any given point in time. Because of this, we cannot pay equal attention to everything at any given moment. Complete unity / togetherness (or complete separation / detachment) with everything implies that everything is giving and receiving energy (everything is attending and being attended to) completely equally all of the time. In fact the giving and receiving are so equal that there is no distinction between the giving and the receiving part at all. Diagram 4 in Figure 2 also illustrates this state of complete harmony. Although this state is associated with complete unity in Figure 2, it can also be associated with complete detachment as well. Both states are characterized as a complete balance of giving and receiving. Although we may be able to experience states extremely close to this at times, it is never complete harmony.

REAL LIFE

Let's step away from the theoretical stuff and move back to real life again. It was mentioned earlier that in real life, there is never complete harmony or complete separation. Life is existence, constant change, constant motion, constant interaction, and constant adjustment. No moment is exactly the same as the next. In the same way, a person in one moment is never exactly the same as in the next moment. As mentioned earlier, we need to pay attention to as much as we can and adjust to these changes each and every moment of our lives. And in this way, we are constantly in a rhythm of giving and receiving.

Although we cannot "not give and receive", we can choose how much we give and receive to some extent. What kind of relationship do you want to have with other people? Do you want a rocky and rough relationship or do you want a smooth and fine relationship? Most of us would prefer a smooth and fine relationship but how do we achieve that? We achieve this by paying attention to other people as much as we can and adjust to these people each and every moment of our lives. If we don't respect and pay attention to others and do whatever we want to do for a while, you can imagine what will happen. People are not going respect you. People are not going to pay attention to you. It is human nature to stop attending to others who do not attend to us. It is human nature to stop respecting people who do not respect us.

Again, the key to a smooth relationship is to pay close attention to everyone that you have a relationship with (which is basically everyone in your life) and respond to them respectfully at every moment of your life. The more you attend to and respect others, the more others will respect and attend to you. Although not everyone will be respectful and attentive to you if you are respectful and attentive to them, the more respectful and attentive you are the more likely the other person will be respectful and attentive toward you. This is the true meaning of "love thy neighbor" and "being respectful toward your fellow citizens". It is a simple formula for relationship success but we often forget to apply it in our real lives. We all have the tendency to take more than we give. Sometimes we take so much more than we give that it seems like we are "stealing" energy.

THE STEALING OF ENERGY

How do we end up stealing energy? You may have learned in biology class that we have a certain level of glucose (sugar) level in our blood that we need and if our supply of glucose becomes lower than that, we look for something to eat to replenish our energy. Similarly, we all have a certain amount of psychological energy that we need and if our supply becomes lower than that, we look for ways to replenish the supply. There are times when we feel like we have given away a large amount of psychological energy and need to replenish our supply of psychological energy. These are the times when we feel stressed, frustrated, lonely, sad, or extremely bored, any state that you don't like and feel you want to change. Basically, we are low in energy. We need to replenish it. All of us have developed various ways to replenish ourselves with energy. Some of us may yell at others in frustration, some of us may criticize others, some of us may eat excessively, some of us may go on shopping sprees, some of us may consume alcohol, tobacco, or other drugs, some of us may throw or destroy things. There are many ways to replenish energy.

Since we are on the topic of interpersonal relationships, let us examine the ways we try to replenish our energy interpersonally. When we yell at others or criticize others, we are dominating and controlling. We are disrespectful towards the other person and we are not attending to the desires of the other person. We take much more energy than we give. If we use the words of the writer James Redfield, we try to "steal energy" from people[2]. We steal energy when we take or receive excessive amounts of energy without giving back much. As long as we do something that makes us feel that we are being respected more than someone else, we are taking energy.

When we are low in energy, we often try to dominate and control other people. All of us have developed habits of dominating and controlling other people in some way. When we are young, we develop habits of stealing energy (taking excessive amounts of energy) from others and they are repeated throughout life like a repetitive pattern. We can learn these patterns using a combination of two things; by trial and error and by modeling. For example, if a baby is crying and is not attended to for a while, what does the baby do? Usually the baby starts crying louder. Let's say that the parents do not attend to the baby when the baby is crying with a soft tone of voice but attend to the baby later on when the baby cries louder because now it is more noticeable and perhaps more disturbing to the parents. If this happens repeatedly in a parent-child relationship, what does the baby learn? The baby learns that he or she only receives attention when he or she cries very loudly. Translated into energy language, the baby learns, "I can only replenish my energy if I become very upset and demand attention from others." In this example, the baby has learned a way to steal energy by trial and error.

We can also learn ways to steal energy by modeling. Suppose a child sees his father yelling at his mother in order to control her behaviors. Yelling at someone to control his or her behavior may be considered to be an act of stealing energy because you are demanding (taking) much more attention and respect than you are giving. By observing his father, the child may try this on other children in the playground to control them. In this example, we can say that the child learned to steal energy from others by modeling his father's behavior (and by trial and error in the playground).

Regardless of how we acquire these behavior patterns, all of these habits of stealing energy are learned. In most cases, these habits continue throughout life and we repeat the same patterns of stealing energy with other people as long as we do not become consciously aware of them (once we become conscious of them, we try to change them because we feel bad doing this to other people). Although we do learn some new methods or new variations of stealing energy as adults, many of them (especially the extreme ones) stem from early experiences in life. Through the insights of various psychologists, novelists, playwrights, and non-fiction writers, I have identified some of the most common patterns of stealing energy from other people[3]. All of us can identify using most of these regularly (or at least in certain times) in our lives.

High maintenance / high expectations
Examples: "Look at me! Listen to me! Love me!"
"I need you to be like this and do this, this, and this"
"Why can't you be like _____?"
This behavior is characterized as being overly demanding of others. We expect others to be the way we want them to be regardless of how that person feels.
Underlying Message: I want you to live up to my expectations

Interrogation / criticism:
Examples: "Did you do what you were told to do?"
"You are an idiot!"
"Those people don't know what they're doing."
This behavior is aimed at making others seem inadequate by being critical of them (by interrogating or criticizing. This makes us feel better than others.
Underlying Message: You (or they) are not the way I (or we) want you (or them) to be and therefore you (or they) are not as good as I am (or we are).

Intimidation / anger:
Examples: "Go to your room right now!"
"You don't want to mess with me!"
"Do this! Or else…"
This is aimed at making others fear the self with intimidation and/or by expressing anger.

Underlying Message: You must be the way I demand you to be. You have no other choice.

Self-Pity / guilt trip
Examples: "My life is so terrible. This is what happened (or is happening) to me…"
"Fine! I will do it myself!"
This behavior is aimed at making others feel sorry for the self or feel guilty for not being compassionate.
Underlying Message: You are making me suffer even more if you don't attend to me

Buttering up (the Boss)
Examples: "I am not very good at this but I know you are. Can you do it?" or "You are so good at this! Can you do this too!?"
This is when we make people do things that we do not want to do by telling them that we are not good at it and/or they are better at it. This behavior is sometimes directed toward making other people feel good about themselves so that they will do things for us.
Underlying Message: I don't have to do these things as long as you do them for me.

Aloofness / charisma
Examples: "……" but looking concerned about something
"………" but looking like you have something up your sleeve
"I am telling you…nothing is wrong, there is no problem!"
"Well…nothing…I can't tell you this."
This behavior is aimed at making others interested in the self by holding out information.
Underlying Message: I have something that you want but you can't have it.

Chainchatting
Examples: "Blah blah blah blah blah" nonstop

This is when we speak incessantly without listening to others. We demand attention incessantly without letting others have their turn. Underlying Message: You should pay attention to me. I am more important than you.

Yes, I know but…
Examples: "What do you think" or "What should I do?"……"Yes, I know but you see…"
This is when we ask for suggestions and advice and but never accept the suggestion or advice from others. We respond to the suggestion or advice by expressing that the suggestion or advice is not what we are looking for. The purpose is not to solve the problem but to receive attention and feel superior.
Underlying Message: Try to help me. I know you can't. I am always one step ahead of you.

Passive Aggression
Examples: intentionally forgetting to do things, saying or doing annoying things,
intentionally making mistakes, faking an illness, clowning around
This is when we do things primarily to cause an emotional reaction (e.g., concern, annoyance, anger, laughter) in someone else. By engaging in these subtle types of behaviors, we receive attention from others.
Underlying Message: You better keep an eye on me. You don't know what's coming next

Avoidance
Examples: "I have to go now." not listening, not responding, avoiding interaction
This is when we avoid others who we feel are likely to steal our energy. This is not a method of stealing energy but rather a method to protect the energy that we have. It helps us avoid having energy stolen from us.
Underlying Message: You can't steal energy from me.

Although there are countless methods of stealing energy and avoiding having energy stolen from other people, these are some common methods that we often see in ourselves as well as others in our everyday life. It is important to note that it is much easier to notice this in the behaviors of others than in the behaviors of our selves. This is largely because the act of stealing or taking energy is not socially desirable. Because it is not socially desirable, we have the tendency to deny that we do this at all. Even when we notice these behaviors in ourselves, we have the tendency to rationalize the undesirable act so that it seems justifiable. Therefore, it is important to note that even though we are not consciously aware that we are taking or stealing energy, we all do this quite frequently.

Please keep in mind that stealing energy is only an extreme form of receiving or taking energy. The difference is only a matter of degree and not of quality. If we take excessively, it is often considered to be stealing of energy. If we only take or receive a little bit, it is considered taking or receiving energy. A relationship that is made of giving and receiving energy is a relatively smooth relationship. A relationship that is made of stealing energy and having energy stolen back is a relatively rough (or rocky) relationship. Different relationships develop different characteristics and these characteristics can sometimes change over time. Let's examine how these relationship patterns develop.

THE DEVELOPMENT OF RELATIONSHIPS

Many of our interactions are ruled by social norms about how one behaves. We should behave in this way in a restaurant and we should behave in this way at a business meeting and we should behave in this way at church and we should behave in this way in the classroom. These social norms, commonly referred to as scripts or frames determine how we should engage in the giving and receiving of energy in certain situations[4]. We learn this primarily from our experiences of actually being in these types of situations ourselves, through reinforcement and punishment as well as modeling the behaviors of other people in similar situations.

In addition to learning the social norms of the larger society, we also develop our own personal patterns of taking energy within those social norms. We all have our favorite patterns of stealing or just receiving energy and use them repetitively throughout our lives on certain people. Although we use these personal patterns within the social norms of the particular situation, it is our unique way of taking energy from other people. For example, I may constantly ask questions as a student in class to receive attention (i.e., take energy) from people in class. Since asking questions seem to be part of the social norm in a classroom setting, it is a legitimized behavior. However, it is my unique way of taking energy from others given the social norms of the circumstances. We usually do this only to certain people because these are the people who allow us to use these patterns on them. Therefore, I may only ask lots of questions in a particular class where I have a particular teacher who allows me to constantly ask questions. Because certain people allow us to use these patterns on them, we are often attracted to these people. Here is how this works.

If we look between the lines when we are interacting with each other, we find that there is a lot more going on than what we can tell from the objective meaning of the words that we are actually saying. In interpersonal interaction, we are constantly negotiating about the nature of the relationship. For example, when you meet and interact with someone for the first time, we are essentially negotiating how we should structure the giving and receiving of energy in the relationship. In the beginning, we often try our favorite ways of receiving or taking energy (we all have our favorites). We try one thing, and if it works, we subconsciously think, "OK, I can take energy from him/her in this way. I like this. I will keep interacting with him/her in this way." If it doesn't work, we try something else. If that doesn't work, we try something else until we find something that does work. If we find something that does work, we are attracted to the person as long as we can repeat this pattern of stealing or taking energy from him or her. For us, that other person becomes something similar to a person that always feeds the dog from the dog's perspective. You want to stay with that person because he or she keeps feeding you (whether it is food or energy).

At the same time, the other person in the interaction is doing the same thing as well. He or she is trying out many of his or her patterns of taking or stealing energy on the other, looking for ones that work. If both individuals find a pattern of taking or stealing energy that works, they will be attracted to each other and continue their respective patterns of taking or stealing and the relationship goes on. If only person A finds a pattern that works, then person B will pull away. This is a natural reaction because even though person A may not mind taking energy all of the time, person B will be exhausted and overwhelmed giving away energy all of the time. If neither of them finds a pattern that works, neither of them will want to pursue the relationship. So if a relationship is to last, both person A and B have to find a way to keep receiving and giving energy to each other equally. Thus, whether you are aware of it or not, in every relationship we have, there is an unwritten agreement concerning how we allow each other to take our energy. On the one hand, it is a wonderful thing to develop relationships of giving and receiving. On the other hand, we need to keep in mind that when we develop relationships, we also tend to become dependent on those people to take or steal energy from.

DEPENDENCY & CODEPENDENCE

When we develop patterns to take energy from other people, we become dependent on them. Humans are creatures of habit and we like routine. We all have the tendency to become dependent on certain other individuals to take energy from. For example, if I develop a habit of taking energy from person A, I begin to feel that I need person A in my life because s/he allows me to take energy from him or her. If person A leaves me, I have one less person that allows me to take energy from and this is very inconvenient for me. Now I have to change my routine and search for other sources of energy. Because I don't want to bother changing my routine, I want person A to stay with me. I need him or her. In other words, I have become dependent on him or her. Most of our relationships are based on our dependencies of taking energy from others. We form relationships because certain people allow us to take energy from them. We all vary in how dependent we are on other people. On the one hand, if we develop a habit of stealing large amounts of energy from someone, we become highly dependent on them. On the other hand, if we develop a habit of taking only small amounts of energy from someone, we are less dependent on that other person.

As discussed in the previous sections, this is usually a mutual process and both individuals only pursue a relationship if they can receive energy from the other in some way. When the dependence occurs in both directions (both individuals in a relationship become dependent on each other for replenishing their energy), the relationship can be characterized as codependence. While the term "codependence" typically refers to specific types of interpersonal patterns in this type of relationship (in the field of psychotherapy)[5], I will refer to all relationships of this nature as codependence. This is because regardless of the interpersonal patterns we use, we are dependent on each other (for replenishing our energy) and this is precisely the meaning of the term "codependence". Just as there are varying levels of dependence, there are also varying levels of codependence. If we both have an interpersonal pattern of taking large amounts of energy from the other person, we are highly codependent. In contrast, if we both have an interpersonal pattern of taking small amounts of energy from the other person, we are less codependent. The smoother the relationship, the less codependent we are of each other. As you can imagine, having a high level of dependence or codependence may be more problematic than having low levels of dependence and codependence. Let's look at how high levels of codependence become problematic.

EMOTIONAL HIJACKING

Let's consider Jane and Jason's relationship. Jane finds that Jason is very sympathetic and attentive to her when she wallows in self-pity. Jason finds that Jane is very attentive to him when he is aloof and withholds information from her. They are attracted to each other because both of them are able to take energy from each other when they feel depleted. Without being conscious of it, they have established the structure and rules of their relationship. They are both motivated to maintain the relationship because they are now dependent on each other for energy. The more dependent we become on others for energy, the more the individuals need each other but the more potential there is for the relationship to become unstable. Here is why.

As you can imagine, the relationship becomes problematic when both Jane and Jason are depleted of energy at the same time (i.e., when both are stressed and exhausted). Neither of them have much to give but both of them are trying to take energy from the other. I think we have all experienced the ugly things that happen when this occurs. We have a battle of stealing energy from each other. "You attend to me!" "No, you attend to me!" "No, you attend to me!" "No, you attend to me!" Both Jane and Jason are furious for a while because their own pattern of taking energy from the other is not working and then both are in tears after hurting each other so badly.

When we are low in energy, we have a natural reaction commonly referred to as the fight or flight response. Relationship psychologists such as John Gottman refer to this phenomenon as "emotional flooding"[6]. Other scholars such as Daniel Goleman refer to this as "emotional hijacking"[7]. I will use the term "emotional hijacking" coined by Daniel Goleman. Emotional hijacking is a natural neural and hormonal reaction that makes us extremely alert and responsive when we feel we are in danger. This system presumably has enabled our ancestors to survive through various types of dangerous situations. For example, because of this system, our ancestors were not eaten by predators at least before they produced offspring. By being emotionally hijacked, we respond to the danger very quickly so that we are more likely to survive. Although this mechanism has helped us survive, it sometimes impedes us from behaving constructively. The type of responses available to us when we are emotionally hijacked is either to fight back or to escape from the danger. When we are low in energy and someone is trying to take even more energy away from you, we sense we are in danger. Our natural response to this is either fight back and try to take energy from whatever is trying to take energy away from you or to escape the situation so that you are able to retain the energy you have left.

When we are with a person that we are not used to taking energy from or a person that we know will not allow us to take energy from at that moment (e.g., your angry boss), our natural reaction when emotionally hijacked is to look for a way to escape the situation. When we are with a person we are used to taking energy from, our natural reaction when we are emotionally hijacked is to fight back and take energy from the other person. We just do this out of habit. It is a subconscious pattern we have developed. The trouble is, when two people have a habit of taking energy from each other and both people are low in energy and are emotionally hijacked, both are looking to take energy from each other (i.e., fight response) at the same time. And of course, since neither has much energy to give, neither of them can take much from the other.

When we are emotionally hijacked, we also lose sight of the larger picture. We become so emotionally involved in trying to take energy from others that nothing else matters. We fail to see the big picture. We only see things from our own selfish perspective. We only think about why we are right, why we deserve attention and respect and why the other person is wrong and is doing something unjust and unfair. We can't see things from the other person's perspective. We can't see things from a third person's perspective either. So when this happens to both individuals, both have no choice other than to fight for energy. We seldom see any other choice.

But...there is another choice. As Daniel Goleman says, even though you cannot be understanding and compassionate when you are emotionally hijacked, you can take a time out[8]. We can take a time out and wait until our hormones in our bloodstream subside. Taking a time out means to stop interacting with that person completely and focus on something else for a while. It is a good idea to remove yourself from the presence of the other person and do something to help you calm down. You can read, go for a jog, listen to music, whatever you enjoy doing. The time out should last at least 30 minutes (usually more). It takes at least 30 minutes (more in most cases) for your hormones to subside and disappear from your bloodstream (and get you out of the emotionally hijacked state).

This time out gives you an opportunity to return to an objective state of mind that enables you to see the big picture again. We become able to see things from the other person's perspective as well as a third person's perspective. This state of mind enables you to be understanding of the other person and compassionate about the other person. This enables you to communicate with each other with respect again. This communication allows you to come to a deeper understanding of each other. This also enables you to see things objectively as an outsider as well sometimes. Most importantly, this enables you to have a smooth relationship with the other person again. In many cases, we feel silly that we were fighting at all when we reach this state of mind. I will explain how this works from a theoretical standpoint in a later section. Before I explain that, I'd like to mention that it is important to keep in mind that this is a simplified picture of what really goes on in the real word because there are more than two people in anyone's life.

RELATIONSHIPS INVOLVING MORE THAN TWO INDIVIDUALS

Although what I have explained about two person relationships in the former sections is accurate for the most part, the actual picture is a little more complex than this. Any relationship involves more than two people. These unique patterns of taking energy develop not only between two people but also among larger groups of individuals. For example, person A develops a pattern of stealing energy from person B, and person B develops a pattern of stealing energy from person C and then person C develops a pattern of stealing energy from person A. In this way, everyone in the group loses energy to a different person and steals from a different person. Energy moves like currents in the ocean. This works with much larger and more complex groups. For example, person A may steal energy from both person B and C and person B may steal energy from person A and D and person C may steal energy from person B and D and person D may steal massive amount of energy from person A. As long as everyone has a way of replenishing his or her energy, the system is maintained.

This is also why we sometimes have situations where person A is comfortable with person B only when person C is around. When one of these people is not involved, the energy does not circulate properly and therefore, one person or numerous people end up depleted of energy. Those individuals who know they will end up feeling depleted of energy in a certain situation, intuitively sense this and thus, try to avoid these types of situations.

In sum, the giving and receiving of energy is very real and it motivates us to do or not do almost everything in our lives. Sometimes, we feel stuck in a pattern and feel like we cannot get out of it (the currents just keep moving). We feel like the energy currents are too powerful for us to do anything about it. How can we change our patterns that we do not want? To explain this, we need to examine this from a slightly new theoretical perspective.

OPEN AND CLOSED PORES

Although stealing energy from others energizes us and provides us with temporary relief, we do this at the expense of others. If we steal energy (take excessive amounts of energy), the other person loses energy and feels worse than before. Therefore, by making ourselves feel better we are making others feels worse. As you have noticed, these patterns of stealing energy do not make for a positive relationship. When we look at our lives, many of our relationships are not much more than repetitive patterns of stealing energy (taking excessive amounts of energy) from each other. Many of them consist of taking turns stealing energy from each other. We taking massive amounts of energy and then give away massive amounts of energy. In essence, we are having rocky relationships. Now that we see what is going on, we know why it doesn't look pretty. So let's change this! Let's stop stealing energy from each other. Let's go from a rocky relationship to a smooth relationship. How do we do that?

The ocean analogy is very useful in explaining this. Let's think of ourselves as hollow entities with numerous tubes as walls around it (see Figure 4). The numerous tubes form a shell around us to protect us from the dangers of the outside world just like our skin protects us from the outside world in some ways. The tubes around us are filled with air so that we can float on the ocean water. Let us also assume that there is some space between the tubes so that water and air can pass through us quite freely. Figure 4 provides us with a two-dimensional diagram of this image and the tubes are represented as doughnut shapes around a hollow opening representing the person. There is nothing but air or water in our bodies and we can increase and decrease the thickness of the walls on the outside of the tubes but cannot increase of decrease the amount of air in the tubes. The thicker we make the walls on the outside of the tubes, the smaller the space between the tubes. Making our walls thicker has numerous effects. It gives us the illusion that we are big and tough (the reason why it is an illusion will be explained later). It also makes air and water inside and outside of the person flow through less freely. It also makes the person heavier and makes the person sink deeper into the water.

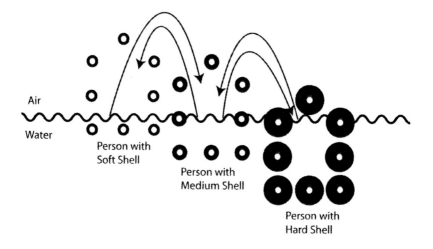

Figure 4. The Ocean Analogy

In contrast, the thinner we make the walls on the outside of the tubes, the larger the space between the tubes. This makes air and water inside and outside of the person flow through more freely. This also makes the person lighter and makes the person rise to the surface of the water. Each entity represented by tubes and the hollow space inside represents one person. The air represents energy and the water represents the absence of energy. We will refer to the openings between the tubes as "pores" and the material on the outside wall of the tubes as "shells". When we "harden our shell", we make the shell thick and the pores small (relatively closed). Conversely, when we "soften our shell", we make the shell is thin and the pores large (relatively open). Furthermore, just as we can never cease to interact with the environment, we can never completely close our pores.

According to this ocean analogy, the point of the game is to have as much air and as little water in your body. Because we can never completely close our pores, this means that we must stay afloat. The more air we have in our body, the more energy we feel, the more water we have, the more depleted of energy we feel. A person can open or close his or her pores by softening or hardening his or her shell as much or as little as he or she wants. The more we harden our shells and close up our pores, the more we constrain the air and water from traveling in and out of our body. This makes it difficult for water to come inside and deplete you of energy (at least temporarily) but it also makes you sink deeper into the water because we become heavier (due to the thick heavy shells). However, because we are deeper into the water, water eventually seeps in from the bottom and makes us somewhat depleted of energy (remember we can never completely close our pores). In contrast, the more open our pores are, the easier it is for the water to flow in and out of your body. As mentioned before, the air represents energy so the more air your have inside of you, the more energy you feel you have. When we have a lot of air (or energy) in us, we are able to relax and open up our pores because we are not afraid of running out of air (i.e., filling up with water). The less air we have inside us, the more afraid we are of running out of air and the tendency we have as humans is to close up our pores to protect ourselves from water coming inside us.

When we take energy from others, it is like taking water from inside our body and pouring it into someone else's body. It is the act of dumping our own water into someone else. The more open the other people's pores are, the easier it is to dump water into them. If we give energy to others, it is like having water poured into our own bodies from another person's body. Thus the more water we give to others, the more energy we are taking. Because the water we had inside us is less and the water inside the other person is more when we pour our water into someone else, we have more air than before and the other person has less air than before. This makes us feel like we gained energy and makes the other person feel like they have lost energy (at least temporarily). This is the experience of taking or receiving energy.

Here's the dilemma of social life. If you close up your pores, you are more likely to protect whatever air (i.e., energy) you have inside you since the air within is more constrained to stay inside you and it is difficult for others to pour water into your body (i.e., others to take energy from you). At the same time, however, you also sink deeper into the ocean and eventually the water seeps inside and the air escapes to the outside of your body (depleting you of energy). If you open up your pores, you are able to stay afloat and thus are able to have more air inside you. However, having open pores also means that it is also easier for others to pour water into your body (i.e., others to take energy from you). As living beings, we not only have a natural rhythm of giving and taking energy but also a natural rhythm of opening and closing our pores. We have a tendency to open and close our pores depending on the how the circumstances around us change. When we are in a safe and trusting environment, we tend to open up our pores and let the water and air flow through us freely (just as we open our hearts to others when we feel safe). When we are in a dangerous environment that makes us fearful, anxious, and insecure, we close up our pores to protect whatever we have left inside (just as we become defensive when we are afraid).

To sum up, we tend to close our pores under two types of circumstances; when others pour water on us (i.e., take our energy) and when we sink deeper and water begins seeping in from the bottom (although neither of them make sense in the long run). We tend to open our pores under two types of circumstances as well; when we have lots of air inside and when we feel unafraid of anyone or anything dumping water on us (i.e., safe environment). When our pores are open, we usually feel fine and relaxed. When we are filled with water or when we are in danger of losing lots of air, we feel like things are rough and our relationships are rocky. We feel anxious, defensive (self-protective), sometimes angry and aggressive, and sometimes sad and depressed. This is when we have our problems. This is when we feel unhappy. Let's examine this further.

When we are either filled with water or in danger of losing lots of air (or both) we become both stingy and greedy and we close our pores and then try to get rid of our water by dumping it into others. Why do we do this? Because we are afraid that something may happen (like others dumping water into us) and we will lose all of our air. This can be understood if we use the metaphor of our relationship with food. When we are afraid of running out of food, we stock up. When we are in this state, we not only protect our own energy but we take energy from others because we are afraid that others will take energy from ourselves and we will run out of energy. Although some are more afraid than others, we are all afraid of running out of energy (or air). What does running out of air mean? What are we all afraid of? You have probably guessed it by now. It is death. Running out of air is like drowning in the ocean. You may not think about this much but our will to live (i.e., maintain our energy) is the same thing as our fear of death. You don't have one thing without the other. They are two sides of the same coin.

Therefore, our nature makes us pour water into each other but at the same time, we need to maintain a certain amount of air inside of us. And so we give and take and give and take so that energy or air (and water) keeps coming in and out of us. In a sense, we all participate in a cycle of energy. Let's have a closer look at how we participate in this cycle of energy.

THE CYCLE OF ENERGY

The problem of closing our pores, sinking deeper, and dumping the water seeping into us onto others is that the other people you dump water into lose air. When others lose air, they are likely to become afraid to lose any more air and tend to close their pores more than before and may even start dumping water onto others (including yourself). By dumping water onto others, you either start or participate in a negative cycle of people dumping on each other, and in many cases, it comes back to you in some way. Here is an example of how this cycle works. Person A dumps water on Person B. Person B dumps water on Person C. Person C dumps water on Person D. And then Person D doesn't have anyone specific to dump water on directly so he bombs a building and kills hundreds of people (and in this way, he dumps water on many people indirectly). A school teacher loses his spouse in this bombing incident and becomes afraid of having more water dumped on him (i.e., Person D indirectly dumped water on the schoolteacher) and dumps water on his students including Person A's daughter who is in his class. Person A's daughter becomes depleted and dumps water from Person A. And then Person A dumps water on Person B..... and the cycle goes on. Sometimes the cycle is smaller. Person A may dump water on Person B and then Person B may dump water right back onto Person A. You give and you take. Or you take and you give. The cycle may be big or small but there is always a cycle and every cycle is a part of a larger cycle. Energy moves like currents in the atmosphere (or ocean) and there is always a continuous flow. Figure 5 is a simplified diagram of how energy flows like currents in the atmosphere from person to person. Some currents are strong and some currents are mild. The stronger currents represent the giving and receiving of radical amounts of energy. The milder currents represent the giving and receiving of smaller amounts of energy. In Figure 5, the thick lines represent strong currents whereas the thin lines represent mild currents.

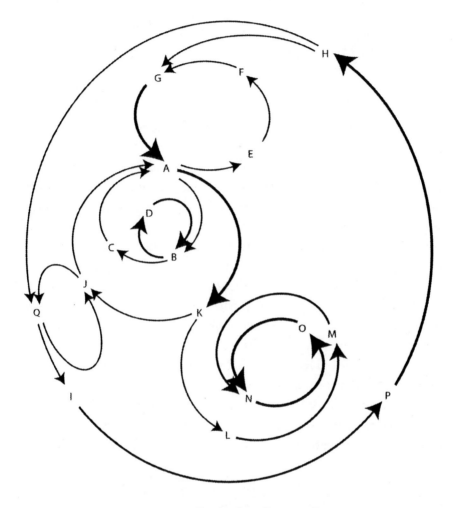

Figure 5. Energy Flowing from Person to Person

This is not to say that everyone who has experienced misfortunes deserves the punishing experience. For example, sometimes innocent people are killed (like the victims of the building that was bombed in the former example). Sometimes, innocent children are abused. Bad things do happen to good people sometimes. People do have a general tendency to steal energy from others who are innocent and less protective of themselves. One bad apple can easily spoil a whole bunch even though one good apple cannot improve the bad apples as easily. The more energy you take from others, the more you are making others lose energy and the more you motivate others to steal energy from others.

What this is saying is that we have a choice to contribute to this world either in a positive or negative way. We are all participants in this world and whatever we do influences everything that goes on in this world in some way. So if you decide to take more energy than you give from many people around you, you may be contributing to making this world full of people who are desperate in replenishing their energy. In contrast, if you decide to live harmoniously and respectfully with everyone in the world, you may be contributing to making this world increase the number of people who are respectful of each other and are able to live in harmony with each other. Now there may be people who take your energy even if you are respectful and attentive to them, and you may not feel the positive effects of your behavior in any immediate way, but by doing this, you are making a small but extremely important contribution to the evolution of the world. You are increasing the chances of this world to move towards more peace, unity and harmony. This is because the more you care, attend to, and respect others, the less energy others lose and the less afraid others will be. Imagine what kind of world we would be living in if everybody in this world made this small contribution. We would have no fights, no hatred, no discrimination, no wars, isn't this what we all really want?

SELF-DEFEATING PATTERNS

As we have seen from the previous section, the solution is not to harden our shells and close up our pores as much as we can when we are full of air. Under certain circumstances, it seems appealing to take as much as you can and then protect it with all your might. Even from an intuitive standpoint, we can all tell that this is not a good solution. Why is it not a good solution? Although the reason for this was explained in one way in the previous section, there are three other ways we can explain why this is not a good solution. First of all, no matter how hard you try, you cannot protect yourself from losing air. As mentioned earlier, we can never completely close our pores because completely closing our pores means that we completely stop interacting with the environment and existence by definition implies interaction with the environment.

The second way to look at it is thinking about what it means to close our pores and harden our shells. Even if you could try to close all of your pores as much as you can forever, the act of closing off your pores will make you tense, anxious, fearful and defensive because you are constantly trying to protect yourself from anyone that may potentially dump water into you. Even though thick shells gives us the illusion that we are big, strong, and tough (i.e., nothing can take energy from us), various psychoanalytic thinkers such as Anna Freud and Alfred Adler have explained to us that it is merely a reflection of us feeling powerless, inferior, anxious, and fearful[9]. Such a state of mind seems like the complete opposite of our concept of happiness. It is a life of anxiety, a life of fear. No one would truly want to live like that for the rest of his or her life.

The third way to look at it is by using the ocean analogy. The very act of hardening our shells makes us sink into the water (i.e., water seeps in from the bottom and we lose air/energy). I think we are all familiar with the irony in this rule of life from our own experiences. Even though we protect ourselves to avoid being hurt, the very act of protecting ourselves is hurtful to us. For example, sometimes we may not socialize with others for fear of others hurting us but the mere act of being unsocial makes us feel lonely, alienated, and depressed. It is a self-defeating pattern. So let's go back to the question. What is the solution? As you can imagine, the solution is in the concept of unity / togetherness.

UNITY / TOGETHERNESS IN THE OCEAN

Ideally, none of us should pour much water on anyone. Unfortunately, as long as we are going to inhabit the same planet (or cosmos) we need to give and take (or receive). As mentioned earlier, as long as we are physical beings we interact whether we like it or not. And as discussed earlier, the answer was not to close up our pores and give as little as possible. It will feel alienating and lonely and even though you and I know that there are some people who have chosen to do this, this is probably not what you want to settle with if you are reading this book. Is there a better answer? I think so. The answer is unity / togetherness.

As we have learned from our discussion earlier using Figure 3, although we can never experience complete unity / togetherness, we can experience things very close to it. Unity / togetherness is closest to a state we experience when both individuals respect each other and are paying close attention to each other at each and every moment of the interaction. It is close to the state we experience when we are interacting with someone and everything is clicking and we feel energized. It corresponds to the right end of the graph in Figure 3. We learned that we can feel energized when we take or receive energy from other people and things. The interesting thing is that we can also feel energized from experiencing unity / togetherness with people and things. And the great thing about being energized from experiencing unity / togetherness is that nobody loses any energy. Everybody gains energy. If you take or steal energy from another person, one person feels good but the other person feels bad. If you experience unity / togetherness with someone, both individuals feel good and energized. This may happen when things are clicking with your basketball team in a game. It may happen when things are clicking when you are having a conversation with someone. It may happen when you are singing together with a group of people. It may happen when two lovers are staring into each other's eyes. Everyone is energized!

How can everyone feel energized? How can we all gain energy (energy) without anyone losing any energy? This was very puzzling to me until I thought of the ocean analogy. I realized that the energy that we feel is not necessarily only the air inside of our tubes. It is whatever air we identify with. It is all in our minds. If I feel a sense of togetherness, I not only feel that the air inside of my body is my energy but the air inside the other person's body is experienced as my energy as well (it is actually experienced as "our" energy). When you feel a sense of unity with someone, you are both sharing the air in both of your "bodies" (as perceived in the ocean analogy). Therefore both people feel energized because both people have more air (or energy) than they did before when they felt like only the air inside their own body was their energy. Now they have the air inside their own body and the other person's body. They feel like they have more air and therefore both feel energized and good.

The image of two people with a thin, soft shell between them in Figure 6 illustrates the experience of feeling unity / togetherness with another person. Both individuals are opening their pores to each other, sharing their air and the air is flowing freely and naturally from one side to the other. Nobody is taking or giving excessively. The giving or taking occurs naturally like beautiful currents in the atmosphere. Neither of them resists the smooth flow of air and neither of them creates any excessive movements by scooping or pouring water on each other. When individuals open their pores to each other, both individuals are attentive and respectful of each other. Furthermore, the open pores enable us to accept and appreciate who the other person is, what the other person does, and appreciate just being with the other person. This sense of unity / togetherness represents the smooth relationship whereas the figure of two people with closed pores dumping water on each other represents a rough or rocky relationship.

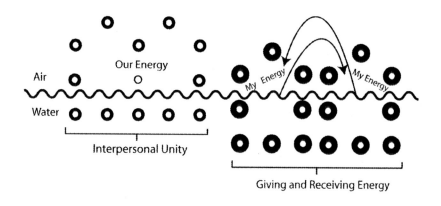

Figure 6. Interpersonal Unity "My Energy/Air is your Energy/Air"
vs. Giving and Receiving Energy

Thus, the smoother the relationship is between two people interacting with each other on the right side (unity / togetherness side) of Figure 3, the more unity / togetherness they feel with each other. In contrast, the smoother the relationship is between two entities indirectly interacting with each other on the left (detachment) side of Figure 3, the less unity / togetherness they feel with each other. However, the smoother the relationship is between two people indirectly interacting with each other on the left (detachment) side of Figure 3, the more unity/togetherness they feel with something else that they are directly interacting with. We become detached with something and move to the left side of the horizontal axis only when we are more engaged (thus we experience more togetherness) with something else. If we are only half engaged with everything, we remain at the middle of the horizontal axis and feel alienated and become very unstable and have rocky relationships with everything around us.

All of this means that the boundary I make between you and I sometimes exists clearly and sometimes does not exist as much when I experience unity / togetherness with you. It suggests that the boundary between you and I is a creation in my mind. I can create it and I can dissolve it. I am free to do whatever I want with it. Let's explore this idea a little more.

BOUNDARIES AS ARTIFICIAL BORDERS

In essence, when we are energized through unity / togetherness, we feel a sense of connectedness and dissolve the boundary between ourselves and the other person in our minds. My air is your air. Your air is my air. Although you rarely notice this, the boundary between you and the other person is really a boundary made in your mind. There is no real boundary there. There is no boundary between you and the air around you and no boundary between you and the chair you are sitting in. It is just a fantastic illusion. In fact, it is such a fantastic illusion that we don't even realize that it is an illusion.

Allow me to explain this from a physical perspective. Physically, what exists are a bunch of molecules. If we break this down further, everything including ourselves is made of a bunch of atoms. An atom has these electrons and neutrons spinning around the nucleus even if we cannot see that happening. The point is that an atom is essentially a bundle of energy and because of that, all matter, including air, is a bundle of energy. Some energy is more condensed than others and so some things feel harder than others. My hand is made of energy more condensed than the air around it so I can run my hand through it without difficulty. My desk, however, is made of energy more condensed than my hand and therefore I cannot run my hand through it. But if I get an axe and swing it at my desk, it may go through the desk and cut it in half. This is because the axe (at least the head of it) is made of energy that is more condensed than the energy that makes the table. Energy of higher concentration feels harder and can go through energy of lower concentration but not vice-versa. But nevertheless, the point is, it is all energy.

If we take another step, we realize that this energy is all connected. I am connected to the air around me and that air around me is connected to the air around you and that air around you is connected to you. So in essence, I am connected to you. There is really no boundary between you and the air around you, or between you and me. We are all connected. You, the air around us, every object around us, all of the oceans, all of the trees, all creatures including you, me, and everybody else as well as the cockroach in the sewer. We are all connected. We are all one. The only reason why we think of ourselves as separate from our surroundings is because we created this boundary in our mind.

We make these boundaries in our minds because they are useful for us when we interact with our environment. It is useful for me to think that I am separate from the chair I am sitting in because then I can expect that the chair will not come with me when I stand up and go to the bathroom. It is useful to know the difference between the soil and the rattlesnake because one of those things can move very rapidly and hurt me much more than the other.

Unfortunately, our mind can only pay conscious attention to a limited amount of sensory information at any given time even though there is constantly a limitless amount of sensory information available both from inside (e.g., stomach churning, heartrate, muscles etc.) and outside our body (in the environment). Because we cannot pay attention to everything going on, we try to pay attention to what we think is important at any given moment. But what we think is important is determined by boundaries. If I think paying attention to my son is important at a certain moment, I need to know where the floor (that he is standing on) ends and where my son begins or which sound is his voice and which is irrelevant background noise. In any case, we are forming boundaries when we pay attention to something. We say that we are paying attention to something because we are paying more attention to it than some other things. In order to do this, we need to specify in our minds the boundaries that separate that something from other things. This is how the mind works. It is a very useful tool but sometimes, it can get in the way of seeing the bigger picture.

The problem is that, after a while, we become so used to these boundaries that we start to believe that the boundary is something real out there and forget that it is just a line drawn in our mind only because it is more convenient for us to think of it that way. There are no lines (i.e., boundaries) out there. There is only a blob of energy. There is only energy that varies in concentration from one place to the other and we are all part of this big blob[10]. Various eastern philosophies as well as many transpersonal thinkers such as Alan Watts and Ken Wilber have explained this idea extensively in their works[11].

FACTORS RELATING TO UNITY/ TOGETHERNESS

Now it seems like unity is unity is unity. But as mentioned earlier, complete unity is an ideal state that we never completely achieve. We can approach unity until we are infinitely close to it but never reach it completely. It is a never-ending road. However, there are various levels of unity (or togetherness). You may experience more or less unity with other people just as you can open your pores more or less. You may feel a sense of togetherness with your child but you also may feel a sense of togetherness with your neighbor. But your sense of togetherness is most likely stronger with your child than it is with your neighbor. How does that work? Earlier on, we defined unity as two (or more) units being deeply and equally respectful (and attentive) toward each other. In a sense, the more deeply and equally respectful your relationship is, the more united one feels. This makes you feel like you understand each other more. Being deeply and equally respectful and attentive means that you have a smoother relationship and that your relationship is further to the right on the diagram on Figure 3. The further right you are on Figure 3, the more unity/togetherness you experience with the other. If we use Figure 4 to explain this, the thinner (i.e., softer) the shell between one person and the other, the more togetherness a person feels with the other (the more we feel that my air is your air).

What are the factors that relate to how much unity we feel? One factor is shared consciousness. Shared consciousness occurs when we share the same perception of boundaries and direction of energy flow. We feel more unity with each other when we can agree that A and B are two different things and that A is now taking energy from B. If one of them sees something different, then there is less unity between the two people. In other words, there is misunderstanding. For example, one of them sees A and B as separate things and the other sees A and B as the same thing, then you have misunderstanding and a much weaker sense of unity.

Lets use a concrete example. Let's say that Peter and Gina are a couple trying to make a living together. They both have a job and they both have separate bank accounts. On the one hand, Peter thinks that he and Gina are two separate individuals and so he puts his income into his bank account and whatever he does with the money is his own business. He feels that he does not have to consult Gina when he uses his money and Gina does not have to consult him when she uses her money. Gina, on the other hand, sees Peter and herself one unit and not as separate individuals. Even though they have separate bank accounts, the money in both accounts is *their* money, not one account for Peter and one account for Gina. Thus, she consults Peter whenever she uses large sums of money in her account and expects Peter to consult her when he uses large sums of money in his account because the money belongs to both of them. Inevitably, Gina becomes upset when Peter uses large sums of money in his account without consulting her. On the other hand, Peter is bothered by Gina constantly consulting him each time she thinks of buying something substantial.

Here we have an example of a misunderstanding between two individuals who do not agree on boundaries. Gina does not see a boundary between herself and Peter while Peter sees a boundary between him and Gina. Thus when Peter spends large amounts of money to buy a racing bike without consulting Gina, Gina is hurt because she feels cut off from the togetherness she usually assumes that she has with Peter. On the other hand, Peter is upset and feels violated when he is asked to go to the store with Gina to choose the right evening dress for her dinner party with her co-workers. This is because Peter sees himself as forced to join Gina and function as one unit even though he sees himself as separate from her.

However, even if two people agree that A and B are separate things, they may not experience a sense of unity if they do not agree on the direction of the energy flow. For example, if two people agree that A and B are different things but one of them interprets an event as A giving energy to B, and the other sees the same thing and interprets the event as B giving energy to A, then there is also misunderstanding. This misunderstanding leads to a weaker sense of unity. Let's look at an example like this.

Let's say Dana and Holly are in a dating relationship. Holly is just getting over a difficult relationship with an abusive spouse who used to bring her red roses all of the time. Dana does not know this and brings Holly some red roses on their date as a kind and caring gesture. Seeing the red roses, Holly is reminded of her former abusive relationship and assumes that Dana heard about her former relationship and was doing this to make her feel uncomfortable. Holly becomes upset at this and as a result, Dana becomes upset because he feels that his kind gesture was not appreciated. Both individuals interpret the same event, Dana giving Holly the red roses, in a different way. Holly interprets this event as Dana taking energy from her. Giving her the red roses was meant to make her feel uncomfortable. Dana interprets this event as Dana giving energy to her. Giving flowers was supposed to represent attending to her desires and caring greatly for her. One interprets the event as energy flowing from A to B while the other interprets the same event as energy flowing from B to A. Again, we have misunderstanding, a lack of unity or togetherness.

Thus the more we share the same perception of boundaries and direction of energy flow, the more we understand each other and the more shared consciousness we experience. The more shared consciousness we experience, the more unity we feel with each other. And the more shared consciousness we experience, the more attentive and respectful we are to each other and the smoother our relationship is. When we attend to each other, we try to understand how the other person perceives things and how the other person feels. Hence, shared consciousness is really the same things as being highly attentive to others and experiencing a deep and spiritual sense of unity. To experience a deep sense of unity, we need to experience shared consciousness and deep mutual respect and attention.

There is also another interesting factor that relates to our sense of unity. It is a factor commonly referred to as "common outside boundaries". As many social and cognitive psychologists have discovered, having a common outside boundary often increases our sense of unity with each other[12]. This is experienced when the boundary between you and another person (or any two entities) becomes less evident (demands less attention) because a common outside boundary that the two of you have with something else is more evident (demands more attention). For example, two people who are often fighting may team up when they face a common enemy (forming a common outside boundary) more powerful than either of them alone. Your family members may argue and bicker at each other during your every day lives but may unite and stick together and protect each other if a violent intruder breaks into your home. This occurs because the presence of a violent intruder forces your family to pay attention to a common outside boundary between all of your family members and the intruder. As a result, the boundary between you and your family members becomes less important and dissolves while there is a common outside boundary demanding more of our attention.

This sense of unity develops when the boundary between you and me demands less attention than the boundary between our group (you and me put together), and someone (or something) else. A good example of this type of unity may be the unity we feel with our fellow citizens of a nation. We may argue with our fellow citizens and we may not be extremely respectful of each other all of the time, but we feel a little bit of togetherness with them just because we are citizens of the same nation. This is especially true when we are at war with another nation. Because the boundary between our nation and the enemy nation is something that we pay lots of attention to, the boundary between the individuals within our nation receives less attention. In a sense, we can see this as shared consciousness at a relatively shallow level.

The essential ingredient for the experience of unity / togetherness is having compatible desires. The more our desires are aligned with each other, the unity we feel with each other. The more we align our perceptions of boundaries, the more our desires become compatible with each other. The more we align our perception of energy flow, the more our desires become compatible. When we get to the point where our desires are not only compatible but very similar (or almost identical) to each other, we experience a deep sense of unity. When I want what you want, we attend to each other and help each other and do things together to realize our desires. When we can agree on our boundaries and perceptions of energy flow, we naturally develop similar desires. When we have similar desires, we feel a sense of unity / togetherness. This is one of the big reasons why we are attracted to people who have similar interests. This is why we tend to form bonds with people who like the same things such as baseball teams, political parties, and types of food. These things enable us to pay attention to similarities in our desires. These things enable us to feel unity with each other.

As you can see from the examples of people who like the same baseball teams and political parties, this type of unity is not restricted to unity between two people. Unity can be experienced with a group of more than two people. In addition, the giving and taking of energy can be experienced not only between two individuals, but also between two groups of individuals. Let's explore this a little further.

GROUP UNITY AND GROUP CONFLICT

Until now, we have primarily been focusing on two person interactions and unity between two people because it has been easier to explain. We know that many of our relationships involve more than two people, whether at work or at home with your family or elsewhere. We can also experience a deep sense of unity when we experience unity and togetherness with more than one person or one thing. We can feel at one with two or three of fifty other people instead of one. If we do feel a deep sense of unity with more than one other person, we usually feel more energized than the unity we feel with one person. In fact, the more people we feel unity with, the more energized we feel and the deeper our sense of satisfaction. This type of group unity is illustrated in Figure 7, where three or more people share the same air in their bodies. The more people we feel united with, the more water we feel we have. Therefore, we feel more energized when we feel united with more than one person. Feeling unity with many people involves experiencing more shared consciousness with many people, having smoother relationships with the people in the group, and we feeling highly energized. In our everyday lives, we feel we belong to many groups defined in many ways, family, group of friends, co-workers, religion, race & ethnicity, gender, nationality, etc. Some of them overlap and some of them are inclusive of other smaller groups as can be seen in Figure 8. The idea that we belong in these groups makes us feel like we are not alone and this makes us feel energized. Furthermore, the more we feel united with our groups, the more our boundaries (between ourselves and members of our group) dissolve and the more energized we feel (i.e., the shells between ourselves and others become thinner).

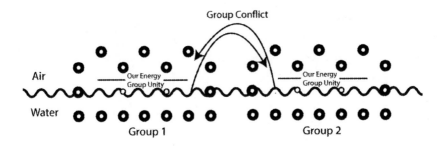

Figure 7. Group Unity and Group Conflict

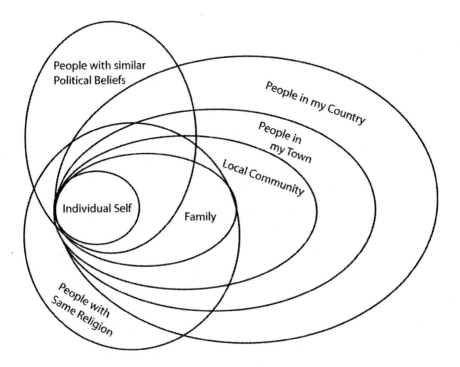

Figure 8. Various Levels of Group Identity

As discussed previously, the experience of group unity can sometimes become deeper when we experience a common outside boundary that demands considerable attention. Two competing political parties may unite and fight against a common enemy (such as a foreign country trying to take over one's land) in times of war. When this happens, the two groups align their desires with each other (e.g., conquer the common enemy) and experience not only more shared consciousness but also feel more respect for each other.

As we can see in Figure 7, we can also have group conflict. Two groups engaging in conflict is analogous to two individuals engaging in conflict. Instead of two individuals stealing energy from each other, two groups are stealing energy from each other. This is essentially what happens in any kind of group conflict, whether it is political conflict, conflict between street gangs, or war. What essentially happens is that two groups become afraid of losing energy and try to take each other's energy. Groups fight for power and fight for energy just like individuals do. And when two groups find peace with one another, they respect each other and attend to each other's desires. When this happens, the two groups experience a sense of unity with each other in the same way two individuals experience a sense of unity with each other.

COMPLETE TRANSCENDENCE

When we are able to experience complete unity in all of our relationships (i.e., with everything in the cosmos), then we experience complete transcendence. We have learned to dissolve all of the boundaries in our mind. When you reach this state, you feel like you are everyone and everything. Everything and everyone is you. You treat everything with respect and attend to its desires. You treat the world like you would treat yourself. This is the ultimate goal of consciousness, and thus the ultimate goal of you and me and everything that exists in this cosmos. In contrast, some Eastern views conceptualize this as being "nothing" instead of identifying with everything. It is the same thing. When we are nothing, we cannot differentiate ourselves from anything else either. When we are nothing, we do not do anything out of our own will either. It is like allowing the water and air to flow freely in and out of you without any resistance (see Figure 9). When we are in this state, anyone can pour as much water into you as they like since the water will seep back out through your pores. You never feel de-energized. Since the point of identifying with everything is so that we do not differentiate ourselves from anyone or anything else, identifying ourselves as nothing is essentially the same as identifying yourself as everything.

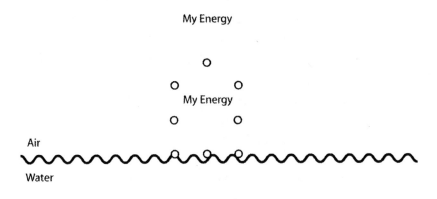

Figure 9. Complete Transcendence

The goal of this game is to try to approach complete transcendence. When we reach that state, there will be no you and no me, there will be no dogs, no trees, no mountains, no oceans, no rivers, and no planets, and no galaxy. There will be no happiness, no sadness, no excitement, no anxiety, no time, no laws, no language, and no countries. There will only be nothingness. There will be none of these things because these things only exist when there are boundaries. The concept of the dogs exists because we experience things that are not dogs. If we understand the concept of dogs, we are essentially learning what things fall into this category of dogs and what things don't. In other words, learning what dogs are is the same thing as learning to tell the difference betweens things that are dogs and things that are not dogs. You have learned to draw a boundary between the experiences of different kinds of objects. The same thing happens when we learn any other concept. The concept of sadness exists because there are times we are sad and there are times we are not sad. If we all felt sad all of the time, the concept of sadness would not exist because there is nothing to distinguish it from. In the same way, if everyone in the world were Italian, then the concept of being Italian would not exist. The concept of Italian exists because there are people who are Italian and people who are not Italian in the world. Time is also created by boundaries. The concept of "the present" exists because there is a past and future. The concept of three o'clock exists because there are times when it is not 3 o'clock. All concepts are used to differentiate our experiences and therefore all concepts are made of boundaries. And if we reach complete transcendence and dissolve all of our boundaries, then there are no concepts. There is no need for words to represent these concepts. No need for thought because all things we think about require the use of concepts. Even though we cannot accurately describe complete transcendence in words because words themselves represent concepts, the closest description of this would probably be complete nothingness[13].

In many religions and philosophies, this state is the state commonly associated with the soul or spirit or the divine. The divine being is in this state of mind and therefore s/he is everywhere and in everything (or nowhere and in nothing) and is timeless. This is because the soul, the spirit, or the divine being transcends all boundaries. Many religions consider the concept of heaven as something similar to this. Everyone is in harmony with everyone and everything and it is full of love, care, and respect. Thus the idea of developing ourselves and approaching complete transcendence is analogous to approaching the spirit of the divine. We are on a road to getting to know the spirit not only in a conceptual way but also by empathically and experientially connecting with the spirit of the divine.

As you can imagine, this idea of complete transcendence is an ideal state of mind and probably not something that can be fully achieved as long as we physically exist. We automatically form boundaries and interact with the environment by engaging in a rhythm of giving and receiving. We cannot completely avoid this. However, we can develop and move to a state of mind infinitely close to this. We can learn to interact with everyone and everything in a smooth manner rather than a rough manner. We can move from the middle to the right side of the diagram in Figure 3. We can try to do this by developing all our relationships (with everyone and everything) toward one characterized by deep mutual respect and attention. This is one of the great challenges of life.

COMPLETELY COMPLETE TRANSCENDENCE

You may have noticed the inherent contradiction in this explanation of complete transcendence. If complete transcendence is a state of no boundaries, why are we distinguishing between harmony and disharmony, smooth relationships and rough relationships, transcendence and non-transcendence. This distinction should dissolve if we achieve complete transcendence and we should not be concerned about approaching one end and escaping the other. In fact, the earlier description of complete transcendence is not actually completely complete transcendence. It is something close to total transcendence, but there is one more step in order to achieve a completely complete transcendence. Complete transcendence occurs when you identify with and are in harmony with everything and everyone. Completely complete transcendence occurs when you go beyond that. You realize that there is no you. Therefore, there is nothing to identify with and nothing to be in harmony with and nothing to interact with. You are not your body, you are not your mind, you are not the cosmos. You do not exist. Completely complete transcendence is just accepting whatever is being experienced and letting everything and everyone be the way they are. When you realize this, it doesn't matter if you have a relationship, it doesn't matter if you are in harmony or not, and it doesn't matter if you have reached transcendence. Nothing matters. There is no good and there is no bad. Everything just is.

Some people may say that this is dangerous because this may allow people to steal and kill and do terrible things because nothing matters anymore. In fact, even if people did those seemingly terrible things, it wouldn't matter to you if you are experiencing completely complete transcendence. If you are experiencing this state, it would not matter to you if someone was killed or if someone was robbed. It wouldn't even matter if you were robbed or killed because you don't distinguish life from death and you don't distinguish your property from another person's property. Moreover, if you are experiencing completely complete transcendence, you would not be motivated to kill or steal because it does not matter to you if someone is dead or alive, and it does not matter to you if you take something or if you don't. It should make no difference to you if you are experiencing completely complete transcendence and thus the idea of doing anything like that or (doing anything for that matter) would never cross your mind.

We have discussed unity with other people so far but you may have noticed that the idea of experiencing unity with not just *everyone* but also *everything* has crept up in the recent sections. This is because we experience unity with not only other people but also other things (non-human entities).

UNITY WITH NON-HUMAN ENTITIES

As much of the previous sections have hinted, we can also have relationships with non-humans such as dogs, cats, insects, reptiles, bacteria, viruses, or plants. If you respect and attend to the desires of a bear in a forest by not provoking them, they will respect your desires and will not attack you or take anything from you. If, however, you do not attend to and respect the desires of the bear, the bear is more likely to disrespect your desires and attack you. This happens with our relationships with all kinds of creatures. If you disrespect the desires of some bees in a hive and poke the hive with a stick, the bees will not respect and attend to your desires and will attack and sting you. You give and take not only with humans but also with non-human organisms.

Moreover, we also have relationships with non-organic material as well. For example, you have a relationship with your car. If you attend to it and take good care of it, it will attend to your desires as well by running well. If, however, you do not attend to it by not taking care of it well, it is more likely to disrespect you and become inattentive to your desires by not functioning well. If you give energy to your car, your car will give energy back to you. You are giving and taking with your car just like you give and take with your family members. You have a relationship with objects just like you have a relationship with other people. If you are able to attend to other objects well, they are more likely to attend to you and you will feel a sense of unity with them just like you feel a sense of unity with another person.

Imagine that you have a wooden chair at home. If you attend to it and show respect to it by taking good care of it, you will feel more at one with the chair than if you throw it around and smash hard objects on it and make it break. You can learn to respect it and attend to it if you think of the object as part of you (i.e., if you feel at one with it). If you think of it as part of you, you will naturally attend to it and respect it as if you were treating yourself and the chair will naturally attend to your desires (by staying intact, functioning well, and looking good). If you feel like the chair is not a part of you, you will treat it as something foreign and you will be more likely to be inattentive to it. We tend to care less about things that are not part of ourselves than things that are part of ourselves. People say that people tend to take care of their own car better than a rental car. This is because we think of our car as part of us even though we think of a rental car as a foreign object (i.e., not a part of us). From these examples, we see that interactions with objects can also be examined in the context of energy exchange. In addition, the more organisms or objects you feel at one with, the more energized you feel. The more we share our energy (i.e., air in the ocean analogy) with people, other organisms, and things the more air we see as our own and therefore, the more energized we feel.

One important point here is that feeling a sense of unity with something or someone does not mean that we are in physically proximity to the object or person. We can feel a sense of unity with a loved one living far away. We can feel a sense of unity with objects that are not in our immediate environment. The unity discussed here is not physical unity but psychological unity. Furthermore, because this is psychological unity, we can also feel a sense of unity with anything we can think about such as abstract concepts and procedures. A person may feel a sense of unity with the concept of capitalism or a person may feel a sense of unity with a specific way to fry a pork chop. Feeling a sense of unity (i.e., identifying) with abstract concepts and procedures also energize you as well. It makes you feel comfortable and sometimes even proud of what you believe in. Although we rarely think of having a relationship with an abstract concept or a procedure, we feel at one with it when you feel like the concept or procedure respects your desires (that is why you identify with it) and when you respect the concept or procedure.

Now some of you may be thinking, "Wait a minute! If unity is equally and deeply attending to each other's desires, how can we experience unity with non-organic objects, concepts, and procedures? Objects, concepts, and procedures don't have desires! This guy is stretching this theory a little too thin." And you are absolutely right. It is a stretch to think that objects, concepts, and procedures have desires. This theory only makes real sense if we apply it to the things that we conceptualize as having desires such as humans, animals, and perhaps even plants (they desire water, light etc.). To move one step further with objects, concepts, and procedures, we need to develop this theory to the next step. And to move this further, we need to examine how the mind works a little more.

ANXIETY AS A RESULT OF DIFFERENTIATION

Earlier we discussed how the mind works by differentiating our experiences. We also learned that we experience more anxiety when we feel we have less energy (or air in the ocean analogy). One of the things that happen in the mind when we experience anxiety is a certain type of differentiation. Anxiety occurs when we experience conflict and conflict occurs when we differentiate two states. The first state reflects our own desire. It is what we want. Sometimes it is described as what we expect or what we think should or ought to happen. It can also be in the past tense. It may represent what we wanted or what we think should have or ought to have happened. In any case, it is representative of what we want (i.e., our desire). The second state represents the real experience. It is what is happening, what has happened, or what might happen. When these two things do not match (i.e., what we want & what has, is, or might happen), we experience conflict and this conflict causes anxiety. The diagram in Figure 10 illustrates the simple difference between conflict and no conflict.

No Conflict - No Anxiety

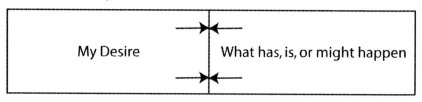

Conflict - Anxiety

Figure 10. Differentiation and Con ict/Anxiety

When we cannot accept what actually happened, we are holding on to what we wanted (our desire). We identify with what we want (our desire) and we separate it from what actually happened. This is the state of not being able to accept our painful experiences. For example, if a coworker says something negative about me, I may say, "I hate him. He is a jerk!" What I really mean here is, "I wish he did not say that about me." In this case, I am separating what I wished had happened and what actually occurred. And I am holding on to my desire (what I wished had happened) and refusing to accept what actually happened. In extreme cases, I may even deny or repress what happened and not even acknowledge that it actually happened. Either way, I am holding on to my desires and refusing to accept what happened. And either way, I am experiencing anxiety at some level. When I repress and deny, I may experience anxiety at a subconscious level. When I just feel upset about what happened, I experience anxiety at a conscious level.

This type of separation in the mind can occur when thinking about future events as well. If I separate what I want in the future (my desire), and what might happen, I also experience anxiety. Although it makes us experience anxiety, creating this separation about future events can also be very useful. It helps us plan for the future and make our wishes come true. If I wish to go to Orlando (my desire) rather than Miami (what might happen) for my vacation even though I have tickets to go to Miami, I can change my flight ticket so that I can go to Orlando rather than Miami. If I think that I'd rather avoid being sunburned (my desire) rather than being scorched by the sun this afternoon (what might happen), I can wear sunscreen or stay in the shade to avoid the sunburn. Being able to plan for the future makes us feel like we have some control over what will happen and the anticipation of being able to control the future makes us feel excited in some cases. This is because excitement is experienced when we are relieved from anxiety or when we anticipate the relief from anxiety. Controlling things really means relieving yourself of anxiety. In contrast, not having control means you cannot relieve yourself from the anxiety you are experiencing (i.e., you lose energy).

Excitement is nice but we must be careful not to get carried away with having a feeling of control over things. There are two reasons why we need to be careful about getting carried away with controlling things. The first reason is that exerting control over things is often perceived as taking or stealing energy from the perspective of the other side if the other side is human. If I feel excited about taking control and overpowering another person in an argument, the other person usually feels as though their energy is being stolen. And because the other person feels like their energy was stolen, they are motivated to steal energy back from us afterwards. The other reason why we need to be careful about getting carried away with controlling things is that there is only a very fine line that separates positive arousal (i.e., excitement) from negative arousal (i.e., anxiety and fear). Excitement occurs when there is a possibility that things do not go the way we want but we feel that we have some control over what will happen (i.e., the possible negative outcome is unlikely). For instance, I may feel excited to play my next tennis match, if I feel like I am in control of the outcome (i.e., I can win). But if I think that I am not in control of the outcome (i.e., I might lose), the excitement will turn into anxiety (or fear). In this case I have separated two things; my desire to win the match and what may happen in reality (that I might lose). Whenever I create this separation, anxiety occurs. If I think I can successfully relieve myself of the anxiety, I feel excitement. If I feel like I do not have control over whether the anxiety will be relieved or not, I feel anxiety (or fear).

If on the other hand, I do not have a strong desire to win my tennis match. I do not separate what I want (i.e., I want to win) and what may happen (i.e., I might lose). This makes me less excited but also less anxious about my tennis match. This is because anxiety and excitement can only exist when we separate those two things. If I don't have any desires about what will happen, the future doesn't matter to me and there is no need for me to be anxious or excited about it. Therefore, in order to manage my anxiety level, I need to manage my desires.

MANAGING ANXIETY: LETTING GO OF OUR DESIRES

Excitement is fine since we all enjoy some excitement in life. However, the negative type of arousal (i.e., anxiety or fear) is not very pleasant. How do we minimize this? The simple but not always effective solution is to take control and try to make everything the way you want it to be. By doing this, we make our desire win over what has, is, or might happen. We basically force the side that represents what has happened, what is happening, and what might happen to become the same as what we desire. In other words, we strive to make all of our desires come true. We strive for the "perfect life". We all know from our life experiences that this is an overwhelming task especially if you have many specific desires. Nevertheless, many of us try this. We try to control everything in our lives so that all of our desires are satisfied. If that works for you, congratulations! You have the perfect life! Unfortunately, most of us cannot control everything in our lives so that all of our desires are satisfied. And because we cannot control everything to satisfy our desires, we are upset (i.e., become anxious) when things do not go our way (i.e., our desires and what happened are differentiated). And to escape from this anxiety, we deny or repress (or use any other defense mechanism on) our experiences (the things that really happened). As humans, we have the tendency to try to control things so that our experiences match our desires and if it doesn't, we still hold on to our desires and try to rid our selves from this separation by lying to ourselves (denial, repression, rationalization, etc.) about our real experiences. We all have the tendency to lie to ourselves about what really happened, happens or might happen and hold onto our own desires. Thus to some extent, we all live in a world of our own (a fantasy world consisting of things the way we want to see it). We get rid of the separation by abolishing the wrong side, the real experience. Although this takes us away from the real world, and we still experience anxiety at a subconscious level when we lie to ourselves, it is a coping strategy used by all of us to some extent.

The milder version of this phenomenon is seen in all of us. It is our tendency to only pay attention to information that is consistent with our own beliefs or distorting our perceptions so that are experiences stay consistent with our beliefs (commonly known as defense mechanisms). The extreme version of this phenomenon is manifested in various psychological disorders where a person has lost touch with the real world to the extent that he or she can no longer participate in the conventional social system. Because we cannot avoid interacting with the real world, this coping strategy produces more problems than it solves because it takes us away from effectively interacting with and adapting to the real world.

If we try to understand this through the ocean analogy, it is as if we harden our shell so that we are influenced as little as possible from the world outside (because we cannot accept what has happened, is happening, or might happen). Letting the water in is like accepting what happens in the real world and letting our real experiences influence us. The more we harden our shell and refuse the water to come in, the more we are resisting our real experiences. The more we do this, the harder our shells become and the more we sink into the ocean. And eventually the water seeps in from the bottom. This water seeping in from the bottom represents the anxiety lurking in our subconscious mind when we use defense mechanisms.

The other more difficult but effective solution is the "Zen" solution. It is to let go of the other side. We can get rid of this separation by letting go of our own desires. If we can let go of what we want, we just have whatever happens left. There is nothing to contrast the real experience (i.e., whatever happens) with. Being able to accept what happens is the same as letting go of what we want. If we can let go of what we want, there is nothing to fear and there is nothing to feel dissatisfied about. In other words, there is no need for anxiety. If we can let go of what we want, we can naturally accept whatever happens. If we cannot let go of what we want, we separate what is really happening (or what happened or what might happen) from what we want (our desires) as long as these two things do not match. It is like thinking, "I wanted this to happen but this happened (or is happening) instead", or " I want this to happen but I'm afraid something else might happen". We are separating our desires from what is, has or might occur. And as long as we have that separation, we experience anxiety (even though some of it may be in the form of excitement).

Medard Boss has extensively discussed the concept of "Gelassenheit". It is a German word that means "letting things go"[14]. He states that most of our troubles are caused by not being able to let go of our desires. Instead of letting go of our desires, accepting the things that happen, trusting people and things and allowing things to take its course, we typically try to control things, repress things and steal energy from people because of our anxieties. If we can just let go of our desires, we can free ourselves from our anxieties.

This seems to be the purpose of crying in response to painful experiences. Although we do not necessarily have to cry for this to happen, we are able to let go of what we have been hanging onto (i.e., our desires) when we cry. And when we let go of what we desire, we can accept our painful experience (i.e., the thing that happened that we did not desire). Crying is the process of saying good-bye to a part of our selves (i.e., what we desire). It is a process of saying good-bye to our old self (which includes our desire) and accepting what happens and allowing the real experience to influence us. This is probably why the Hopi native tribe have a proverb that translates, "Don't be afraid to cry. It will free your mind of sorrowful thoughts."

In order to let go of our desires, we must trust that things have turned out the way it is for a reason and that things will turn out all right without us having to control it. It is like learning to allow water to be poured into us without hardening our shells. If we can allow water in without hardening our shells, the water will eventually seep out and we will eventually have lots of air again because we are able to stay afloat. In other words, if we have faith and hang on to our hopes and remain patient, the storm will eventually subside. We must trust the nature of things and respect its way and not try to control it (i.e, not harden our shells and dump out the water). Only then can we rid ourselves of our anxieties. Only then can we stop water from seeping in from the bottom. Only then do we really stop losing air (i.e., energy). Only then can we transcend our boundaries. Being completely transcendent is the same thing as having no desires at all. We do not resist. We do not control. We accept things just the way they are. It is a state of having no conflict at all. To sum up what we have discussed in this section, I have created some simple illustrations in Figure 11 to describe the two ways we typically use to get rid of our inner conflicts that cause anxiety.

Conflict - Anxiety

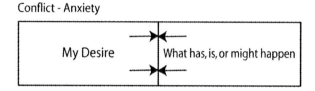

1. Taking control to make our desires come true

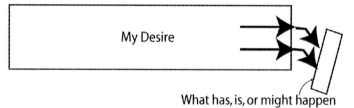

2. Letting go of our desires and accepting whatever happens

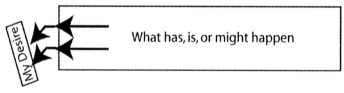

Figure 11. Two ways to reduce Anxiety

MY DESIRES VS. WHAT HAS, IS, OR MIGHT HAPPEN: MYSELF VS. OTHERS

How does this relate to giving and taking in a relationship? What does the separation of my desires from what has, is, or might happen mean in the context of a relationship? When we have a relationship of giving and taking with someone, the relationship we are experiencing is not directly with that person. The relationship is in our mind. We are actually separating our desires from what has, is, or might happen and my self represents my desires and the other person represents what is, has or what might happen. The conflict is not really between my self and the other person but between my desires and what the other person did, does, or might do (i.e., what has, is, or might happen). If the other person does something that is not consistent with my desires, I feel like the other person is taking my energy. In this case, we feel like we have lost energy because my desires are losing the battle between "my desires" and "what has, is, or might happen" and I feel that the other person represents "what has, is, or might happen". And because the other person represents "what has, is, or might happen", I feel like the other person took my energy. If the other person does something that is consistent with my desires, I feel like I am receiving energy. This is because my desires are winning the battle between "my desires" and "what has, is, or might happen" and the other person represents what has, is, or might happen. If we both do things that are consistent with both of our desires, we both feel like we are receiving energy. This is when we both feel energized. This is the experience of interpersonal unity. This is why we feel unity with people who have the same desires as we do. When I do something to satisfy my desire, the other person feels like their desires are being satisfied as well.

What this tells us is that our relationships with others are a reflection of the relationships between our desires and "what has, is, or might happen" in our minds. Whenever we experience a conflict with others, it is a reflection of conflict within ourselves. Conflict of any kind is a sign that our desires do not match what has, is, or might happen and that we are holding onto our desires and resisting what has, is, or might happen. We will discuss how these inner conflicts relate to our outer conflicts in more detail in a later section. To illustrate how this relates to what we have discussed in the previous sections, I have created some illustrations in Figure 12 to describe how our inner conflicts are perceived as conflicts in relationships with other people (as well as other

No Conflict - No Anxiety

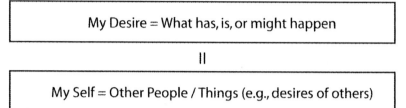

Conflict - Anxiety

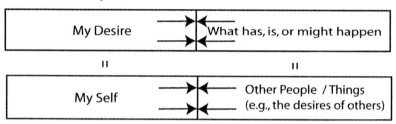

Giving and Receiving of Energy

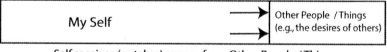

Self receives (or takes) energy from Other People / Things

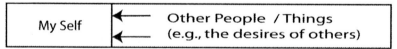

Other People / Things receive (or take) energy from Self

Figure 12. Correspondence between Internal
and External Relationships

As you may have figured out by now, this relates to our relationships
with non-human objects in the same way. For example, let us say I have

a relationship with my car (i.e., a physical object). I experience conflict with my car when I separate my desires with what has, is, or might happen in relation to my car. The conflict is not really between my self and the car but between my desires and what the car did, does, or might do (i.e., what has, is, or might happen). If the car does something that is not consistent with my desires (e.g., it stalls), I feel like the car is taking my energy. In this case, we feel like we have lost energy because my desires are losing the battle between "my desires" and "what has, is, or might happen" and I feel that the car represents and "what has, is, or might happen". If the car does something that is consistent with my desires (e.g., the car starts and after stalling), I feel like I am receiving energy. This is because my desires are winning the battle between "my desires" and "what has, is, or might happen" and the car represents what has, is, or might happen.

Now I may be attentive and respectful of my car and periodically change the engine oil of my car and do many other things so that it keeps running well. When I do this, I may feel like I am giving energy to my car because changing the engine oil is not something I personally enjoy (i.e., not my desire) and thus "what has, is, or might happen" (e.g., the car might break down) seems to be winning against "my desire". When I accept what might happen if I don't change the engine oil and allow that thought to influence me (e.g., the car may break down), I feel like I am giving energy to my car (because my car represents what might happen). But I also feel that because I gave energy to my car, the car gives energy back to me by doing something that is consistent with my desires (e.g., running well). And because the car does not really have its own desires that I need to behave consistently with, I may even feel a sense of unity with the car when it is just doing something consistent with my desires.

How does this relate to our relationships with abstract concepts? For example, let us say I have a relationship with the concept of democracy (i.e., an abstract concept). I experience conflict with democracy when I separate my desires with what has, is, or might happen due to democracy.

The conflict is not really between my self and democracy but between my desires and what happens due to democracy (i.e., what has, is, or might happen). If I am a dictator and the concept of democracy is introduced to the people in my country and it motivates people revolt against me, the revolt is not consistent with my desires. When this happens, I feel like democracy is taking my energy. In this case, I feel like I have lost energy because my desires are losing the battle between "my desires" and "what has, is, or might happen" and I feel that the concept of democracy represents "what has, is, or might happen". If on the other hand, I as a dictator destroy all of the books and slaughter all of the people that introduce the concept of democracy to our citizens, I may feel like I am taking energy from the concept of democracy. This is because my desires are winning the battle between "my desires" and "what has, is, or might happen" and the concept of democracy represents "what has, is, or might happen".

In contrast, I may be attentive and respectful of the concept of democracy and study it and allow it to influence my governing style. In this case, I may not experience conflict because my desires are consistent with what is and might happen. I desire to become a democratic leader and this is what might happen. I do not need to take nor give with the concept of democracy because I am democracy now. When this happens, I am in unity with the concept of democracy and it is even an important part of my identity. This is very similar to a situation where we feel very close to a group of people and that group is an important part of our identity (e.g., I am a Roman Catholic).

How does this relate to our relationships with procedures? For example, let us say I have a relationship with a new way to make fried dumplings (i.e., a procedure). I experience conflict with the cooking method when I separate my desires with what has, is, or might happen due to the cooking method. The conflict is not really between my self and cooking method but between my desires and what happens due to the cooking method (i.e., what has, is, or might happen). If I am trying to make fried dumplings that taste like the delicious ones I had at the

Chinese restaurant and make fried dumplings using a new recipe that I found in a magazine, I may be afraid that the dumplings will not taste as good. In other words, what I desire may not match what might happen. If I feel like the dumplings will not taste as good as I desire, it means that I feel like what might happen (i.e., the dumplings might not taste as good) is going to win over what I desire (i.e., the dumplings taste just as good as the one's in the restaurant). In this case, I feel like I am losing energy because my desires are losing the battle between "my desires" and "what has, is, or might happen" and I feel that the new magazine recipe to make fried dumplings represents "what has, is, or might happen". If on the other hand, I discard the new magazine recipe and make the dumplings using a recipe from the chef in the Chinese restaurant so that I feel like it will taste just as good as the ones in the restaurant, I may feel like I am taking energy from the new magazine recipe. This is because my desires are winning the battle between "my desires" and "what has, is, or might happen" and the new magazine recipe represents "what has, is, or might happen".

In contrast, I may feel like the new magazine recipe will allow me to make the dumplings just as good as the ones in the restaurant. In this case, I may not experience conflict because my desires are consistent with what is and might happen. I do not need to take nor give energy with the new recipe because I feel like the recipe is consistent with my desires. I am in unity with the new recipe. I am at peace with it.

In sum, the quality of the relationships we have with other people and things are reflections of the quality of what goes on in our mind. If we are in conflict with other people or things, it is a sign that we are experiencing internal conflict in our mind. If we are at peace in our relationships, it is a sign that we are experiencing peace in our mind. It is very simple. Perhaps it is too simple that we often fail to realize this. It is important to remember, however, that it is not completely in our mind. Our relationships are real. The desires of other people are real. If we do not respect and attend to the desires of others, they will most likely feel depleted of energy and they will be less likely to attend to your desires. Although you can choose to have certain desires or not, your desires do actually influence how you behave and influence other people. And thus thinking about relationships in terms of giving and receiving energy is still a very useful tool. Furthermore, because we have relationships with non-human objects (as well as concepts and procedures), we can also become dependent on these things as well. The next section focuses on dependence and addiction to non-human objects from the perspective of giving and taking energy.

DEPENDENCE AND ADDICTION ON NON-HUMAN OBJECTS

Earlier, we discussed dependence and codependence in human relationships. Being dependent on someone means that we have developed a habit of receiving energy from that someone and therefore we feel that we need that someone in order to maintain our energy (since changing our routine requires extra effort and energy). Just as we can develop relationships with human entities, we can also become dependent on non-human entities. People sometimes become dependent on animals such as pets because they allow us to take energy from them. We can tell our dog to sit, regardless of whether our dog wants to sit or not. We can play with our dog when we want to and ignore our dog when we are busy doing something else. In essence, we are forcing our dog to attend to our desires more than we are attending to the desires of our dog. This means our dog is allowing us to take energy from him/her. We develop habits of taking energy from our dog and therefore we feel that we need our dog. Although this is not always the case, because we as the owner of our pets have more social power than our pets, we do run into the possibility of becoming highly dependent on our pets.

We can also become dependent on non-organic entities such as our car or computer. If we know how to handle them correctly, oftentimes we feel like we can do what we desire with these objects. It makes us feel like we are in control. We can make it do whatever we want it to do without attending to it very much. In relationship terms, the car or computer typically attends to our desires more than we attend to it. This makes us feel powerful and in control. Whenever something allows us to feel powerful and in control, we feel like we are receiving energy. In human relationships, we feel powerful and in control when we receive energy. In the same way, we are receiving or taking energy when we feel powerful and in control interacting with objects. Many of us have developed routines controlling these things to the extent that we feel like we can no longer live without our car or computer. In other words, we have become dependent on those objects. In many cases, they are the things we conceptualize as "our toys" and we become dependent on them.

We can also become dependent on objects that we ingest or inhale such as various types of food, alcohol, tobacco, coffee, tea, and all kinds of other substances. This is what we commonly refer to as addiction. Although there are some other effects that accompany these types of behaviors, we are essentially doing what we desire with these objects by ingesting or inhaling them and this makes us feel like we are in control. Many of us smoke when we are low in energy (under stress). Although smoking has a psychological effect due to the chemicals being inhaled, it also makes us feel powerful. We usually smoke because we want to. It is perceived as our own desire that we are attending to. When I take a break to have a cigarette, it is "my time" and it feels like "my time" because I am doing what I desire during this time. This is also why some of us overeat when we are upset (i.e., low in energy). It makes us feel powerful and in control since we are doing what we desire. This is also why some people may break things out of anger. It allows us to feel powerful when we do what we want to with the things around us. The broken object is attending to our desires. My desires are in line with what might happen (i.e., the object will break). In contrast, if the object does not break, our energy level goes down more and we feel frustrated because my desire does not match what is happening.

Doing these things to energize us temporarily allows us to take energy from the environment. Sometimes we develop a habit of overeating, smoking, or breaking things, etc. When any of these behaviors become a habit, it is a form of dependency. We end up feeling like we cannot live without that object (or that type of object). We feel like we must have the object for us to cope with anxiety. Ideally, we'd like to minimize our dependencies as much as possible. Ideally, we'd like to become transcendent and minimize the taking of energy as much as possible so that we can experience harmony with our environment. As noted earlier however, we must give and take energy to some extent with the environment as long as we are alive.

THE INEVITABLE GIVING AND TAKING OF ENERGY

The concept of transcendence is important in our understanding of things and we can experience states infinitely close to complete transcendence (and perhaps something like complete transcendence for temporary moments) but as long as we are alive, we have a mind and as long as we have a mind, we have boundaries. This is just the way our mind functions. And as long as we have desires, we cannot avoid losing energy. We desire to maintain our energy, and we desire to stay alive. But things happen in life. We have accidents, we have misfortunes, we feel hurt, and we get hungry etc. These things are inevitable to some extent. You cannot live your whole life without ever being disappointed, dissatisfied, fearful, or anxious.

And because of this, we cannot avoid taking energy from the environment either. It is fundamentally necessary for us to survive. For example, we need to eat in order to survive. Eating is a form of taking energy. We do it because our desires have to be attended to. The desires of the food we eat are not attended to when we eat them. The chicken you ate for lunch did not want to be eaten. It wanted to stay alive and walk on the soil and eat and mate and so on just like us. When we eat it, we are not respecting and attending to the desire of the chicken. We are in a sense taking energy or rather stealing energy. The same applies to any kind of meat, seafood, vegetables, grains, and fruits. They are all living beings. None of them want to be eaten and digested by other organisms. When they are eaten, it is against their desires. Since we cannot avoid eating, we cannot avoid stealing energy. We can also dis-respect the desires of non-organic matter. Breathing is an example of this. When we breathe we break down oxygen molecules so that we can use it as energy in our body. The oxygen (O_2) molecules did not want to be broken down. They are sticking together because it feels right for them that way. That is why they have the tendency to stick together. In this way, we are disrespecting its desires by breaking it down and using it for our own energy.

As the well-known philosopher, Arthur Koestler has explained so insightfully in his work[15], the world is organized in whole/parts called holons. Everything in the universe is a whole made of smaller parts as well as a part of some larger whole at the same time. Certain things (energy/matter) have a tendency to stick together and function as a larger interdependent system and form larger wholes and those larger wholes have a tendency to stick together and function as part of a larger system with other larger wholes to form even larger wholes. Each one of those wholes at any level is identified as a holon. A holon at any level has two tendencies. The first is a tendency for self-preservation. The tendency for self-preservation is the tendency to keep its parts together so that it can maintain its integrity. The other tendency is to integrate itself into a larger whole. This tendency is the tendency to unite with other holons and form larger holons. For example, atoms stick together to form a larger system called molecules, molecules stick together to form larger systems such as organelles in our cells, organelles stick together to form a larger system called, cells. Cells stick together to form a larger system called organs, organs stick together to form larger systems such as an individual human. Individuals stick together to form a larger system called families, families stick together to form larger systems called communities. Communities stick together to form a larger system called towns, towns stick together to form larger systems called nations and it goes on and on forever in both directions. Each holon at every level is motivated to keep its parts together to maintain the integrity of its system. For example, you as an individual (a holon, a system) are motivated to keep your organs and tissues together for individual survival. You may have noticed that I have skipped a few levels of holons along the way for simplicity but I trust that you understand the idea. On the one end, you can go smaller than atoms and on the other we can go further into systems larger than nations.

The point is that whenever we break down a holon, we are essentially taking energy. All holons are motivated to maintain the integrity of their system (to have their parts stick together and function together as a whole) under most circumstances. If you break a holon down into its parts (whether it is oxygen molecules, carrots, or communities), you are disrespecting the desires of the holon to remain intact and using the energy derived from breaking down the holon for your own benefit. This is essentially how we all give and take energy with the environment.

The whole point of this theory is that although we cannot avoid taking energy from the environment, we can minimize it as much as possible. We can steal large amounts of energy from the environment and have large amounts of energy stolen back. A worldwide example of this may be the environmental problems we are having. We have spent many years disrespecting the environment and stealing its energy and now the environment is disrespecting our desires and taking back large amounts of energy from us. In contrast, we can take a little and give a little and be respectful of each other and enjoy relatively smooth and harmonious relationships. In order to experience peace and harmony, we must be as respectful to other holons as we can even though being in complete peace and harmony cannot be achieved as long as we are motivated to exist and stay alive. If we go one step further, we realize that there are psychological holons just like there are physical holons. Let's examine how this works.

The Self-System

PSYCHOLOGICAL HOLONS IN HUMAN RELATIONSHIPS

We can take energy from breaking physical objects down into its smaller constituents. We can take energy from non-organic objects such as atoms, oxygen molecules as well as vitamin pills. Just as we can take energy from breaking down an atom to obtain nuclear power, we can also take energy from breaking down organic objects such as carrots and chickens.

Similarly, we can also break people down psychologically and take energy. As discussed earlier, we give and take energy in human interaction. The giving and taking of psychological energy is much more subtle and much less noticeable than the giving and taking of physical energy even though the process is essentially the same. We can take energy by breaking down the mind, the psychological integrity or the self-system of an individual. This is what we do when we take energy from someone. We essentially break down their psychological integrity by telling them, "Your way of understanding and doing things is inadequate. You need to build a new understanding and pattern that incorporates my desires".

As Donald Snygg and Arthur Combs have explained in their work, the main purpose of the mind is to develop our phenomenal field[16]. We all have built an understanding or a system in our minds that enable us to both make sense of the world and to enable us to maintain the energy necessary for us to both psychologically and physically survive. The world works like this and I can do this and this to maintain my energy. In terms of the ocean analogy, I can protect myself from having water leak in or dumped on me and if I do this or if I see things in this way, and I can get rid of my water when I need to by perceiving things in this way and by doing this, this, and this. In a sense, we build a system in our mind and a shell around it to maintain and protect our system. Although Donald Snygg and Arthur Combs refer to as the phenomenal field, many other theorists have used other terms such as self-system, the self, or self-integrity[17]. I will use the term "self-system" because it refers to how the world relates to the self and fits in well with the general systems approach taken here. The more we let someone into our lives and allow them to take energy from us, the more we allow them to influence us and change us. In other words, the psychological integrity or self-system that we had before we allowed them to influence us is slightly broken down because they have influenced us and changed our understanding of the world and how it relates to the self. We now have to find a new way to understand the world and rebuild our self-system. When someone breaks down our self-system and takes energy (energy), our world has slightly changed. We have received new information and therefore the way we used to understand the world no longer works. We must try to makes sense of this new world by changing our understanding of the world so that it makes sense even with the new information that we just received. Because our self-system was broken down, we have released some energy (just like an atom releasing energy when it is broken down). And the energy we have released is commonly perceived to be absorbed by the person who influenced us and broke down our self-system. Therefore, we see this as the other person receiving, taking, or stealing energy from us.

When we break someone's self-system down, the other person usually breaks down our self-system and takes energy back. Each time we interact, our self-system is slightly broken down and we engage in a rebuilding of our integrity so that the world makes sense again. Every time we do this, we slightly change and evolve. Thus interaction is a constant process of change and a constant process of evolution. We repeat the process of slightly breaking down our integrity and then rebuilding it again over and over when we interact with other people as well as other objects in the environment. This is the way we continuously adapt to the social and physical changes in our environment.

The more we allow others into our lives (and influence us), the more we change and evolve. If we build a hard shell and do not let others influence us much, our integrity is not broken down as much (i.e., nobody can dump much water into us) and therefore, little rebuilding (i.e., finding ways to keep or take the water out) is needed. This is what is commonly referred to as "stonewalling". Stonewalling is when we refuse to open up to others. We sometimes refuse to understand what the other person is experiencing at an emotional level. We sometimes do things for others out of defensiveness and there is no sincerity in our actions. For example, we sometimes apologize just to get someone off our backs even when we don't really feel sorry. When we do any of these types of things, we are trying to preserve our self-system (understanding of the world) because we are too anxious, fearful and lazy to change it. It may make life easy temporarily, but we stop evolving and adapting to environmental and social changes. If we refuse to let others influence us, our understanding of the world and our general system of exchanging energy from the environment may no longer be applicable to the world after a while. This may have drastic consequences in the long run by making us fossils that are no longer adaptable to our new social and physical environments.

In relationships, this is how two people can grow apart from each other. They no longer open up to each other and allow the other to influence them in any significant way. Because no person lives in a vacuum, every person interacts with the environment and adapts to the changes in the environment throughout his/her life. If we do not allow the other person to influence us, we no longer adapt to the changes of the other person and the other person plays a smaller and smaller role in our system (because s/he no longer fits into our outdated self-system anymore). You then end up with a system with the other person having a minimal role in it and you no longer have a deep psychological connection (unity/togetherness) with the other person. In other words, the understanding of the world of the two individuals are minimally integrated and there is very little shared consciousness. The desires of the two individuals become less and less compatible with each other. As discussed earlier, less shared consciousness and less compatible desires implies less unity. This is essentially what happens when people grow apart from each other.

Thus, there is a significant degree of difference between paying attention at a superficial level and allowing someone to deeply influence us. We all have frustrating experiences when other people are only half-heartedly listening to us. They may be watching TV or reading the newspaper or just daydreaming about something else while we are speaking to them about something important to us. In these cases, we feel we are not really being heard. This is because we sense that the other person is not allowing us to influence them at a significant level. In other words, they are maintaining their self-system and not allowing us to break it down. They have a hard shell around them and they are not letting us in. We are not receiving energy from them. In order to have a quality relationship where two people truly interact and grow together, we have to let our walls down (i.e., soften out shells) and let the other person in. We need to allow the other person to take energy from us. This is the essence of any real relationship, human or otherwise.

The key is to keep our pores open so that we allow water and air to freely to come in. Every time water is dumped on us our shell has the tendency to harden because we become afraid. When we encounter something we have not dealt with before, it makes us self-protective and afraid. Thus each time something influences us (i.e., we have water poured on), we must find a way to make our shells softer again. And each time we make our shells softer again we develop our understanding of how we relate to the world a little more than before. Each time we find a way to make it softer again we evolve as humans. In contrast, if we do not find a way to make our shells softer, our shell becomes harder and harder as more water is dumped on us throughout our lives.

Although harder shells prevent others from dumping water on us to some extent, we sink into the ocean and the water begins seeping in from the bottom. When water begins seeping in from the bottom we must make an effort to keep scooping water out and dumping it on other people and things. Thus failing to find a way to soften our shells so that new information can influence us not only impedes our development but also makes us dump more water onto (i.e., steal energy) other people and things.

If we look at the ocean analogy and review for a minute, we notice that the water represents anxiety (i.e., lack of energy), the air represents satisfaction, fulfillment, relaxation and calmness (energy). The shell walls represent our defense mechanisms or any mechanism used for self-protection. The more we use these mechanisms, the thicker and harder our shells. We will call these mechanisms "defenses" from now on. In addition, all of the entities with the shells around them that initially represented individual humans can also be representations of objects, concepts, procedures, or anything we else can think about (because we can have relationships with anything we can think about). And finally, the self is whatever we identify our self as at the moment, ranging from just our individual minds to everything in the cosmos. What about the self-system? How can we understand the self-system using the ocean analogy? This is our next topic.

THE SELF-SYSTEM AS A COMFORT ZONE

The self-system is a comfort zone. When we are dealing with people and things that are within our self-system (i.e., people and things you already know how to deal with) we are comfortable. It is like the comfort of being in your own house. You are familiar with the things, and people in it and you know how to interact with them to maintain your energy level. In fact, when you are in your comfort zone, you don't even have to think about your actions. Things just seem to flow in a natural sequence. It is like driving your car on a familiar route. You don't even need to think about how to drive or where to turn. It is automatic. The more comfortable we are, the less we consciously think about our experiences.

Furthermore, the self-system is not restricted to physical proximity. A close friend who lives 6000 miles away may be part of your self-system. We can have abstract concepts and procedures as part of our self-system. For instance, the concept of recycling may be part of your self-system. This may make you feel more comfortable with living in a town that recycles rather than a town that doesn't even though you may not know anything else about the towns. Likewise, a particular procedure to clean the toilet may be part of your self-system. This may make you more comfortable when a toilet is cleaned in a particular way than in any other way. The self-system is the product of the mind and is not a physical entity. Therefore, it is not restricted to Newtonian laws of physics.

When we experience something very similar to an experience we had before, we primarily assimilate the new experience into the self-system because it is very similar to an experience we already had before[18]. In this case, the self-system requires little adjustment and we are not shaken out of our self-system very much. The mind primarily develops the ability to apply the self-system to a wider variety of experiences. When we experience something that requires more accommodation rather than assimilation, we are shaken out of our comfort zone more and we focus our conscious attention more on the new event. The mind does one of three things after this: (1). It may ignore the information if the self-system finds this information irrelevant and unimportant in maintaining our energy level. (2). It may repress or deny the information if the self-system finds the event important but too threatening to the self-system (i.e., the self-system cannot maintain your energy the way it has before if you continue without changing but changing requires too much initial loss of energy). In this case, the person subconsciously knows that it is important to incorporate this information in his/her self-system but is afraid to do so. (3) It may take in the information of the new event and break down our self-system temporarily until it reconfigures itself so that all of the things in the self-system plus the new event become part of the new self-system. Sometimes, the new event is experienced multiple times before it is integrated in the self-system. It may be considered unimportant and ignored the first time and then incorporated later on after it has occurred five times and the self-system decides that it is important. Or, we may initially be too afraid to face the new information but become ready to face and incorporate the information into our self-system later on. Regardless of how it happens, when (3) occurs, we can say that we have gained insight and understanding and a significant amount of learning has occurred[19]. We are now comfortable with the new information. It has becomes part of our comfort zone/self-system.

The self-system includes the word "self" because it is the very thing we identify ourselves with. In the ocean analogy, it is represented as the physical space (part with air and/or water) that I identify with. If I feel a sense of unity with my kitchen utensils, a friend, my driving routine to work, the self includes both the space that represents my individual self and the space that represents with my kitchen utensils, a friend, my driving routine to work. In terms of the ocean analogy, the air inside myself as an individual, my kitchen utensils, my friend, and my driving routine to work are identified as my air (or our air). My interaction (although it may not be conceptualized as interaction since I am in unity with it) with these people, things, and concepts can be conceptualized as air and water flowing naturally in and out among the spaces that represent these things. Basically, I identify my self as anything I feel a sense of unity with (i.e. comfortable with), whether it is a person, object, a place, an abstract concept, or a set of procedures (see Figure 13). And when I am functioning within my self-system, I feel comfortable and do not need to think very much about what I am doing. I am at one with my surroundings and everything in my mind. I am in my comfort zone.

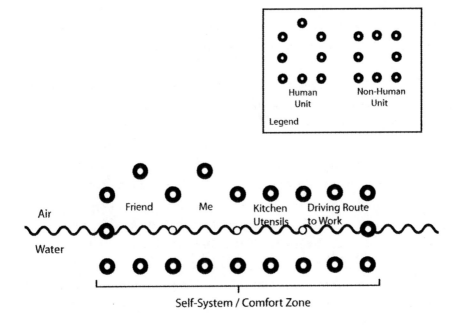

Figure 13. Self-System as a Comfort Zone

When we are in our comfort zone everything seems to flow naturally. Thus, we have expressions like, "being ourselves", and "my world". In sports, we have expressions like "playing within your self" and "playing my own game" which refers to playing in your comfort zone where things flow naturally. When something does not go our way (i.e., the way we expect), we separate whatever we are interacting with from our self-system. In other words, our mind creates a split between our desires and what has, is, or might happen. This split shakes us out of the comfort of our self-system and makes us feel like we are in unfamiliar territory or enemy territory (i.e., territory we do not identify with). This makes us uncomfortable and our anxiety level rises. When this split occurs, we often move from a naturally flowing experience to a choppy self-conscious mode of functioning. We are jolted out of our unity and harmony and we are motivated to take energy. It becomes our desires against what has, is, or might happen. It motivates me to control and dominate the situation so that my desires come true. It motivates me to take energy so that my self-system does not have to be modified.

Lets look at an example and interpret it using the ocean analogy. If my friend is part of my self-system, we are giving and receiving energy with each other smoothly and equally. We feel connected and the water and air is flowing in and out of our bodies naturally. However, when my friend suddenly takes more energy from me than usual, I separate my friend from my self-system and no longer feel comfortable with my friend. I am now defensive and begin competing for energy with my friend instead of sharing energy with my friend. At this point I no longer feel connected with my friend and the air and water no longer flows in and out our bodies naturally like before. Instead, the space representing myself is smaller now and I am motivated to scoop water out of me and pour water on my friend (i.e., take energy from my friend). Thus the boundaries of the self-system can change from moment to moment depending on our state of mind.

The key is to remember that separating whatever we are interacting with from our self-system and becoming defensive is not the only option. We can also do the exact opposite and adjust to our self-system rather than making whatever we are interacting with adjust to our self-system. We can try to allow the experience to influence us instead of becoming defensive and trying to take energy (i.e., control the environment). Sometimes, this works better than becoming defensive. The more we open up to these new experiences and allow these experiences to influence us, the more our self-system grows and the more we can approach a state of complete transcendence. Of course, complete transcendence is a state where the self-system is no longer necessary (since I identify myself as everything or nothing and there is no need to protect or obtain energy anymore). In sum, the self-system is our comfort zone and as long as we can stay in this comfort zone, things run smoothly. The self-system is also highly related to the well-known concepts of self-esteem and self-confidence. The next section briefly discusses how they relate to each other.

SELF-ESTEEM AND SELF-CONFIDENCE

The commonly discussed concept of self-esteem is merely a reflection of how large our comfort zone is. It is a reflection of how much our self-system can accommodate. If we have a self-system that enables us to deal well with a wide variety of different situations, we are able to maintain our energy level in a wide variety of situations. This enables us to stay in our comfort zone more and thus it makes us feel happier with ourselves in general. This is the state of high self-esteem. In contrast, if our self-system is not well developed, we feel like we are outside of the comfort of our self-system more frequently (i.e., we experience the separation between our selves and other people and things more frequently) and thus we feel like we are frequently trying to protect our energy as well as take energy from the environment. This is the state of low self-esteem. This is when a person frequently feels high levels of anxiety because his or her self-system is not developed enough to deal with many of the situations s/he encounters in his or her life. The person is constantly alert and cannot relax because s/he does not have a set pattern to deal with many of the situations s/he encounters. Thus the more a person is able to remain in the comfort zone of the self-system regardless of the variety of situations s/he encounters, the more self-esteem a person has. This is why our self-esteem grows when our self-system develops into more sophisticated systems as we gain more experience.

Self-confidence is very similar although self-confidence is often conceptualized as situation specific rather than a global personality characteristic (like self-esteem). We have self-confidence in situations where we are able to stay within the comfort of our self-system. That is, we are self-confident when we already have set patterns in the way we deal with a situation. We know what to pay attention to and what to ignore, and we have a set pattern on how to respond to the particular things that happen in the situation. When we are in a situation that we are not familiar with, we are jolted out of the comfort of our self-system and we lose some confidence because we have no set patterns in the way we respond to the situation that enables us to maintain our energy level. As a result, we typically try to protect our own energy and take energy from the environment and no longer experience unity with the environment. In order to maintain a sense of unity with the environment even when we find ourselves in unfamiliar situations, we need to understand how attention works.

ATTENTION AND THE SELF-SYSTEM

Let us look at the self-system from the perspective of attention. The more anxious we are, the narrower our attention becomes. Although we do not think of it in this way, the whole idea of focusing our attention means not only paying close attention to certain things but also not paying attention to other things. The more we pay attention to a certain thing, the less we pay attention to other things. On the other hand, the more relaxed we are the more we can pay attention to a wider range of things (i.e., sensations). This relates to how the self-system works.

When we are functioning within our self-system, we know what we need to pay attention to not only certain things but a certain range (i.e., width) of information. It is as if our self-system has a program saying, "In order to maintain my energy level in this situation, I need to pay attention to this, this, and this and I can ignore this, this, and this, and in order to maintain my energy level in this situation, I need to pay attention to this, this, and this and I can ignore this, this, and this ". When something unfamiliar occurs and we are no longer able to maintain our energy level as we used to, we are jolted out of our self-system. When this happens, our natural reaction is to resist the change and apply force to enforce our self-system onto the new situation. In order to do this, we raise our anxiety level and focus (i.e., narrow) our attention so that we can apply more force to certain things (i.e., steal energy). For example, if a door doesn't open we may try to break it open. This reaction is useful in some situations. If we are in a room on fire and the only exit door does not open, breaking a door open may be a reasonable solution. We have inherited this reaction system in our biological make-up from the old days when we needed to fight or run away from a predator or a warrior while we are injured (i.e., in pain/anxiety). Remember, focusing attention on things also means diverting attention from other things. In these types of life or death situations, it sometimes helps to focus (i.e, narrow) our attention and ignore certain things (e.g., ignore the pain from injury), so that we can function in a way that increases our chances to survive. We can focus our attention and apply more force when we are fighting (e.g., when we beat on the predator or enemy warriors), if we defocus our attention from other things. Anyone who engages in sports or any type of martial art knows that mental focus is essential in applying significant force. In a sense, our desire to protect ourselves physically in these life or death situations is analogous to our desire to protect our existing self-system.

However, most situations in life do not require such drastic measures. Most situations in life that jolt us out of the comfort zone of the self-system require us to calm down and pay attention to a wider range of information than usual. As was mentioned in earlier sections about dealing with energy thieves and emotional hijacking, most situations that make you anxious are dealt with more effectively if we calm down rather than becoming anxious and upset. For example, instead of reacting with aggression towards the executives when our project proposal is rejected, we may look at the political and/or financial structure of our organization to see if there is another way to make this project work. Paying attention to a wider range of information is allowing you to see the bigger picture and understanding things from a wider perspective. Paying attention to a wider range of things also allows you to experience unity with more things in your surroundings. The more we pay attention to a wider range of things, the more we increase the chances of having more things attend to us as well. In other words, this increases the probability that you will experience mutual attention and respect (i.e., unity) with a wider range of things. The higher your chances of experiencing unity with a wider range of things around you, the more energized you feel. The more energized you feel, the more relaxed and peaceful you feel and feeling peaceful is a sign that there is no problem (nothing to worry about). It is a sign that you feel that things are alright if you stay within the natural flow of events. In terms of the ocean analogy, it is a sign that you feel that you will never really lose any air if you keep your pores open and allow water to flow in and out naturally.

When we are jolted out of the comfort zone of our self-system, we resist the change and apply force to enforce our self-system on a new situation. Applying force is the same as taking or stealing energy. Taking or stealing energy always involves focusing our attention on something specific to take or steal energy from. When our self-system fails to maintain our energy, we focus (i.e., narrow) our attention. When we focus our attention, we always focus on something within the range of things that our self-system directed us to focus on to begin with. Thus, we fail to notice anything beyond what the program in our self-system tells us. In other words, we are trying force our own self-system onto the new situation even though they are not compatible.

However, when we calm down and pay attention to a wider range of information than usual (wider range than what our self-system made us attend to), we go beyond our old self-system to figure out a way to maintain our energy level in this new situation. In other words, our old self-system breaks down and reconfigures itself so that it is able to maintain our energy level in all situations including the new one. Thus a new self-system that includes and transcends the old system is developed. This repeats itself over and over throughout life so that we are able to make sense of and adapt to an increasingly wider range of situations in life. Therefore, the more we develop our self-system, the wider the range of information we attend to. And the wider the range of information we attend to, the higher our chances of feeling unity with a wider range of things. Therefore, development of the self-system is analogous to developing the conscious ability to experience more unity with a wider range of things.

ANXIETY AND THE SELF-SYSTEM

As you have realized from the previous sections, anxiety is a very important emotion for us. It is a signal telling us that we are or will be in danger. It is an emotion conducive to survival for all animal species including humans. Anxiety makes us alert and highly responsive to the environment. If we did not experience anxiety, we would not run away from dangerous predators or protect ourselves from natural disasters. Without anxiety, we would not protect our children when they are in danger. Without anxiety, we would not protect our food and other resources from being stolen. Anxiety is conducive to survival and enables us to escape immediate life and health threatening dangers. Anxiety is an integral part of our will to survive.

However, anxiety can also cause us many problems, especially with us humans. We discussed earlier that we steal energy and become scavengers because of anxiety. We become avoidant of others because of anxiety. We behave in aggressive and violent ways because of anxiety. We also use defenses because of anxiety. It is this anxiety that makes us refuse to attend to and respect others. It is anxiety that makes us hate others. We experience anxiety because we anticipate pain (and ultimately death). Because pain is such a powerful negative emotion, we try almost everything we can to avoid it.

One of the reasons why anxiety can be so problematic is that anxiety makes us narrow our attention. When we narrow our attention, we fail to see the big picture. When we narrow our attention we become completely involved with our own desires and fail to attend to anything else (e.g., the desires of others and whether our desire is worth holding onto). When we are anxious, our mind assumes that our desires are extremely important and tries everything possible to realize our desires.

In most cases, our desires are "small stuff". Most of our desires are trivial and are not worth being anxious about. It is just that anxiety makes small problems look so big because we cannot pay attention to anything else at the moment. In many ways the key is to calm down and widen our attention so that we see the bigger picture. This helps us notice and become consciously aware of how we have made some problem much bigger than it actually is. When we notice that we are anxious about something "small", it is easier to let go of our desires (the cause of anxiety). It makes us think, "Do I really need things to be this way? Does it really matter?" and we are often able to let go of our desires because the answer ends up being, "No, It doesn't really matter". This may be difficult to do when we are emotionally hijacked, but even when we are emotionally hijacked, we can at least take a time out if we can realize that we are emotionally hijacked. Then after we calm down, we may be able to realize that it is just "small stuff" that we are upset about. Attention and the self-system are also highly related to the commonly used term known as "the zone". As you may have recognized by now "the zone" is really referring to the comfort zone of our self-system, even though it is actually a little more than that.

THE ZONE

When we feel like we are in unity with something that we are not usually in unity with, it is a very special experience. When this happens we are completely focused on what we are doing (even though we were not focused before) and we are actually paying attention to a wider range of things than usual (wider range than what our self-system usually makes us attend to). At the same time, we are responding to a wider range of things at every moment. When this happens, we experience unity (or something very close to it) with a wider range of things than usual. This is why we have the expression, "everything comes together" to describe this type of experience. When this happens, everything seems to be spontaneous and everything seems to flow naturally. In sports, it is often called "the zone". Psychologists like Abraham Maslow use the term "peak experience" to describe this[20]. Mihalyi Csikszentmihalyi calls this experience the "flow"[21]. It is a mysterious experience that feels spiritual in some ways. In fact, some people try to experience this by engaging in spiritual types of activities such as prayer, chanting, or meditation. The important thing here is that, when we are in this state of mind, we are not consciously attending to a wider range of things. It is an subconscious process and it only occurs when we do not differentiate what has, is, or might happen with "what should happen", "what ought to happen" or "what I desire" at all. This is why some people in the world of sports use expressions like "He is completely unconscious!" when a player is in "the zone".

This is similar to the experience of functioning within the comfort zone of our self-system but it is much more energizing. The reason why it is more energizing is because we are not only functioning within our self-system but we are functioning beyond that. We are more relaxed and we are attending to a wider range of things than what are self-system usually directs us to do. Thus we are experiencing unity with a wider range of things than we normally do and thus we feel more energized than we usually do. Our self has expanded beyond our self-system and thus we are functioning beyond our self-system but we have not separated ourselves from what we are interacting with. Even though we are functioning outside of our self-system, we have not switched to our choppy self-conscious mode of functioning characterized by differentiation. We are still functioning in a natural, smooth non-self-conscious flow as if it is all still within our self-system. Even though we are in a situation that seems normally out of our comfort zone, we are still able to remain comfortable. In the ocean analogy, it is like seeing yourself as much more than the space you usually see yourself as. The boundary between your self and non-self has moved further outward. Thus, more air/energy is experienced as "your air/energy".

This experience of our expanded self is not permanent (this is why it is so special). Therefore, the experience of "the zone" is not the same as transcendence and development of the self-system since we eventually return back to our old self-system. It is as if we have temporarily connected with some outside force that energizes us by allowing us to experience more unity than usual. Although some people mistake this experience for transcendence due to personal development because the experience itself is similar, it is not the same. True transcendence due to personal development occurs at a more conscious level and thus enables us to stay there until we move on to the next level of transcendence and development.

As we have seen until now, the self-system allows us to maintain our energy level in a variety of ways. Sometimes, however, the self-system can be problematic. Because part of the function of the self-system is defensive in nature (prevent excessive energy loss), it can sometimes create more problems than necessary. In the next sections we will examine how the self-system can go awry and mislead us in our development.

EARLY EXPERIENCES AND EXTREME INTERPERSONAL PATTERNS

Earlier, we discussed how different kinds of interpersonal patterns evolve in relationships. We learn different ways of receiving, taking or stealing energy throughout our lives. These interpersonal patterns are an important part of our self-system. Our self-system, which includes our interpersonal patterns, develops from our life experiences. Furthermore, many of the more extreme habits of taking and stealing large amounts of energy may be acquired in childhood and tend to stay with us throughout our lives. The reason why we acquire many of the extreme habits early on in life is because we are primarily in relatively powerless social positions when we are babies and little children. As babies and little children, most people we interact with are more powerful than us. During these early stages in our lives, we are dependent on powerful people such as parents and other caretakers for our comfort and survival. A newly born baby cannot feed him/herself. A little child will have difficulty surviving without the support and protection provided by parents and other caretakers. Because we, as little children and babies, are dependent on these people, these people are more powerful than us. They can refuse to feed us, they can refuse to provide us with shelter, clothing, and comfort, and they can even abuse us (both psychologically and physically) if they wanted to. The point is that little babies and children are at the mercy of their parents, babysitters, nannies, and anyone else who takes care of them because they have less social power than most people they interact with.

Because babies and little children are in relatively powerless positions, powerful people tend to take energy from them. Parents say do this and don't do that, teachers send messages saying you will fail if you don't do this. These people are essentially saying "I want you to be the way I want you to be, not the way you want to be. And if you are not the way I want you to be, I will make you suffer the consequences (by punishing you or by not accepting you or not caring for you properly)". And if the less powerful people (i.e., babies and children) manage to take large amounts of energy from those powerful people in some way, the powerful people are in a position to take back even more energy from the less powerful to make sure that they don't do that again. The point is that babies and little children have very little opportunity to take much energy but other powerful people have many opportunities to take energy from them. As a result, these babies and little children end up being low in energy quite often. If other people constantly take large amounts of energy from us and we don't have many opportunities to take energy from anyone, we take as much as we can when we have the chance. This is why we tend to develop extreme habits of stealing large amounts of energy early in life.

The more energy we have taken from us at an early age, the more extreme one's habits of stealing energy become. This is because the more energy people steal from us, the less energy we have left, and the more desperate we become in replenishing our energy. Not only that, we also become constantly afraid that others are going to steal energy from us. The mere fact that we are afraid that others will take energy from us makes us build ways to defend ourselves. And the more we try to defend ourselves, the more anxiety we experience. It is a negative cycle that we trap ourselves in. Many theorists have used various terms to describe this experience of anxiety. Sigmund Freud and Carl Rogers used the term "anxiety"[22] and Donald Snygg and Arthur Combs used the term "threat"[23]. Alfred Alder's widely used term "inferiority" relates highly to this experience as well[24]. When we feel inferior, we feel powerless (i.e., energyless), and when we feel powerless, we feel anxious. I will, for the sake of simplicity, use the term "anxiety".

How does anxiety make us lose energy? The more anxious we are (i.e., the more water we have in ourselves), the more defensive we become by using various mechanisms of self-protection (i.e., defenses). If we use the ocean analogy, all of the defenses we are using are placed in the shell. In fact, the thickness of the shell directly corresponds to the amount of defenses we are using. The thicker our shells become, the more we sink into the ocean and the more we allow water to seep in from the bottom. Because water keeps seeping in even when nobody is stealing energy from us, we constantly have the need to scoop the water out and dump it on other people and things. Thus, the more we try to defend ourselves, the more we steal energy from anything that is considered not part of ourselves. If I am a person who consistently had large amounts of energy stolen, I learn that the world is a dangerous place full of people who are trying to steal energy from me. As you can imagine, having this type of belief system would make a person constantly defensive thinking, "Who is going to steal my energy next?" Because I have acquired this general belief that makes me defensive, I feel I am constantly low in energy (because water keeps seeping in from the bottom) and this makes me steal as much energy as I can whenever I have a chance. This is why highly defensive people steal lots of energy from other people and things (or whatever they can conceptually separate from themselves). I refer to this belief system and behavior associated with it as "scavenging".

SCAVENGING

Because some people have been in unfortunate circumstances where others have consistently taken large amounts of energy from them (especially early in life), they develop this general belief that the world is a dangerous place full of people who are trying to steal energy. These people typically become scavengers. They look for opportunities to steal energy, and when they find them, they steal as much as they can. These people seem to roam around in society looking for prey (people and things to steal energy from) and steal from them whenever they have a chance. They look for people who are kind and giving, they look for people who are in vulnerable social positions, they look for people who are easily taken advantage of, they look for people they can easily steal energy from. They look for people with open pores. The less extreme scavengers, may steal small amounts of energy here and there every once in a while so that they are able to maintain relationships with their prey so that they can keep coming back to them. These scavengers usually have subconsciously developed very sophisticated game plans to steal energy in subtle ways so that their behavior seems socially acceptable on the surface. The well-known psychiatrist, Eric Berne has discussed some of the game plans used by these individuals in his famous book "Games People Play"[25]. The more extreme scavengers may steal large amounts of energy at once from their prey, destroy the relationship (because nobody wants to stay with people who steal large amounts of energy from them) and move on to the next prey.

Unfortunately, the problem that scavengers have is never resolved by taking energy from the environment because these people feel afraid of running out of energy regardless of how much they take. Their mechanisms for self-protection (i.e., defenses) are filled in their shells, making them heavy and making them sink deeply into the water. Because they are deep in the water, the water keeps seeping in regardless of how much they try to scoop out and dump onto others. It is sometimes described as a living hell because they are constantly anxious and thus are constantly low in energy.

Some people call this "fighting your demons" because it is as if these people are constantly fighting to keep the water out (i.e., losing energy). Some people call this "trying to get the monkey off your back" because they are trying to get rid of something but they do not know what it is. Most of the time, they think that the problem is in something or someone else (i.e., something other than themselves) and they try to solve the problem by working on that something or someone else by taking energy from it (i.e., by controlling and dominating it). In other words, they think that someone or something is pouring water into them (i.e., stealing their energy) and that is why they feel so low in energy. They try to solve the problem by pouring the water out of them and back into that someone of something else (i.e., steal energy back). Obviously, they can't get rid of the problem because they fail to see that the cause of their problems is not in the outside world, but in themselves (i.e., their own defenses). The problem is not that others are pouring water into them. The problem is that their own defenses (i.e., self-protective mechanisms) are so abundant and powerful that they make their shells heavy and make them sink into the water (and therefore water seeps in from the bottom). It is their own defenses that are depleting them of energy and not anything or anyone else. That is why we say that the monkey is on our back. We fail to see the monkey because it is behind our backs. It is actually a part of us but we cannot see it. It is like a psychological blind spot. Scavengers keep working on the outside world to fix the problem (by stealing energy from others) even though that is only a temporary solution to the problem (because the water seeps back in) and the monkey never leaves their back. The demon never goes away.

When we feel that we do not have enough energy, we all have a tendency to blame others. We think, "This person is stealing my energy", "This event drained me of energy", "I am not happy because of these things and it is not my fault" and we try to take it back from other people or things because we think that it is only fair to do so. Often times this only provides temporary relief and makes the situation even worse afterwards by initiating and adding momentum to a negative cycle of stealing energy back and forth. In order to deal with this effectively, we need to notice that we only feel that we don't have enough energy when we use defenses. It is our defenses that we need to become aware of and learn to deal with and not anybody or anything else outside of ourselves.

All of us engage in scavenging to a certain extent. We all try to find opportunities to take energy from the environment. We only differ in the how much we do this. The more negative experiences (losing excessive amounts of energy to many people and things) we have, the more defenses we tend to use and the more anxious we are of losing energy, and the more we tend to engage in scavenging. On the other hand if we have experienced many negative experiences but have developed a consistent awareness that the cause of this is in our own defenses rather than some outside force, we may begin learning how to let go of these defenses. Letting go of our defenses means letting go of our desires. Since many of our defenses that cause us to be scavengers stem from the separation between what we desire and what happened in the past, we can let go of our defenses by letting go of our desires. Before we discuss this in further detail, however, let's examine what happens when we respond to our monkeys.

RESPONDING TO OUR MONKEYS

As mentioned in the previous section, when we have many experiences of having energy stolen from us, we develop generalized expectations believing that people and things are very likely to steal energy from us (even if it is not the case). Because we have these negative past experiences, we become avoidant, self-protective, and we scavenge. We basically begin responding not to what is really going on in the world but to our monkey on our back (i.e., our defenses). Even if someone approaches us and tries to interact with us in a smooth manner, we respond by being avoidant and self-protective or by being aggressive and stealing energy from the other if we think we have an opportunity to steal energy. In this way, we respond not to the person that we are interacting with but to our own monkeys, our anxieties, the threats that we ourselves create to ourselves, our own issues, our own anxieties, our own feelings of powerlessness and inferiority. And because we are responding to our own monkeys, the other person we are interacting with sometimes receives an unexpected response. It can be unexpected in three possible ways. Firstly, the response can be unrelated to the present context (e.g., topic of conversation) because the responder is responding to a personal issue (the anxiety coming from his or her personal concern) rather than what the other person said or did. Secondly, the respondent may take back massive amounts of energy (out of proportion to the amount taken by the other person) because the respondent is responding to not only what the other person said or did, but also their own anxieties (caused by their own defenses) on top of that. Thirdly, the respondent may be self-protective and avoidant because s/he expects the other person to steal more energy from him/her.

Let's take the example of Dana and Holly discussed earlier. To refresh your memory, Dana and Holly are in a dating relationship. Holly is just getting over a difficult relationship with an abusive spouse who used to bring her red roses all of the time. Dana does not know this and takes the liberty to bring Holly some red roses on their date as a kind and caring gesture. Seeing the red roses, Holly is reminded of her former abusive relationship and assumes that Dana heard about her former relationship and was doing this to make her feel uncomfortable. Holly becomes extremely upset at this and begins yelling at Dana. In this case, Holly is responding to her own monkey and not to Dana's behavior. Because Holly is responding to her monkey that Dana does not know about, her extreme reaction is surprising and out of proportion to Dana's initial gesture (taking the liberty to bring Holly some roses). Alternatively, Holly may respond by being self-protective and avoidant toward Dana because she associates Dana with her former spouse in her mind and becomes afraid that Dana may also be abusive to her.

Even though some people may have more than others, we all have monkeys on our backs. One of the challenging tasks of life is to face those monkeys buried in the subconscious part of our minds and learn to let go of them. Learning to face and let go of our defenses requires tremendous courage and considerable effort but we always notice that it was worthwhile after we have learned to let them go. We almost always feel this way afterwards because it improves the psychological quality of our lives. We feel we are free and light because the heavy shells (filled with our defenses) are not weighing us down anymore. This is why we use expressions like "the weight being lifted off our shoulders" and "getting rid of our emotional baggage". This makes us float higher in the ocean and enables us to have more air and less water in our system. This also means that our pores are more open and this implies that we feel that the air inside of us is more connected to the air around us. All in all, this means that we experience much more energy and feel much better in our every day lives.

You may recall that one of the possible responses in the example above was Holly to yell at Dana. Yelling at others as well as all other forms of stealing energy is considered to be aggressive behavior. And since stealing energy is considered to be a response to anxiety, aggressive behavior is also considered a response to our experiences of anxiety.

In other words, any time we behave aggressively we are showing others that we are afraid or excited which, as discussed in earlier sections, are two sides of the same coin.

AGGRESSION AND AVOIDANCE AS A RESPONSE TO ANXIETY

Aggressive behavior is another term for stealing energy. We are behaving aggressively when we burst in anger and intimidate others, when we criticize or belittle others, control others, or physically hurt others. Any act of aggression (or stealing energy) is always a response to a loss of energy. Whenever we are aggressive, we are trying to replenish the energy we lost. This is somewhat related to situations where we are avoidant or feel inhibited in any way. We are protecting ourselves from losing energy when we are avoidant and we are replenishing the energy we lost when we are aggressive. When we are low in energy and feel we are in a situation where we can steal energy and get away with it, we steal energy by becoming aggressive (dumping out our water into someone else). However, when we are low in energy and find ourselves in a situation where we have no hope in stealing energy and getting away with it, we become avoidant. Therefore, whenever we are avoidant, inhibited, angry or acting aggressively in any way, it is always useful to ask ourselves, "What am I afraid of?" or "What is the anxiety behind my avoidant or aggressive behavior?" and "What are the defenses I am using to get rid of my anxiety?" As long as we keep reacting to our anxieties by stealing energy, we can never let our defenses (e.g., denial, repression etc.) go. And because we can never let our defenses go, we can never stop feeling anxious and thus keep responding with aggression or avoidance. In other words, as long as we avoid facing (becoming consciously aware of) the monkey, the monkey remains on our back. We must examine our defenses (i.e., our monkey) by figuring what desires we are holding on to and let go of those desires at the root of our defenses. Only then can we begin to get our monkey off our back and stop sinking. Only then can we feel truly fulfilled (with energy / air) in our lives.

How do we get the monkey off our back? Because our aggressive and avoidant reactions are commonly subconscious processes, the first task here is to become aware of one's reactions of aggression and avoidance. Then we must examine the defenses (what we are denying or repressing) behind those reactions and figure out what desires we are refusing to let go. Once we can let go of those desires (what we wanted), we can accept what happened and integrate what happened into our own self-system.

Let's look at an example. Jamie is now an adult, but has repressed some memories of being abused by his father as a child. Jamie constantly uses defenses (e.g., repression) to deal with his unacceptable past experiences. Because he is using powerful defenses to shield himself from his painful experiences, his shells thicken and water seeps in. As a result, he constantly feels low in energy and behaves aggressively toward the people around him by yelling at them and making hurtful (aggressive) remarks (i.e., stealing energy). From the previous sections we learned that we are rarely aware of why we are reacting to certain things in certain ways. We usually steal energy from others without the awareness of what is really happening. We are not aware of why we are doing this. We are not even aware that we are actually stealing energy in most cases. Similarly, Jamie may react in this way without being aware of what is causing this behavior. The aggressive behavior is just an automatic, subconscious, and natural reaction acquired through past experience.

In order for Jamie to develop out of this pattern, Jamie first needs to become aware of his aggressive reactions. Then he needs to become aware of the anxiety underlying the aggressive reactions (i.e., what am I afraid of? what am I repressing?). In the next step, he needs to figure out the discrepancy between what he desires and what happened. In the final step he needs to let go of his desires so that he can accept the painful experience (i.e., what happened). The nature of the defense is to not allow what happened (or what is or might happen) into one's self-system because it does not match what one desires. Once he accepts that painful experience, it eventually becomes incorporated into his self-system after a period of reorganization. This requires allowing the experience to break down his self-system that he had without the experience of abuse (when he was repressing it) and then rebuilding a self-system that includes the painful experience. This means accepting what happened without comparing it to what should have or what he wished would have happened and rebuilding his understanding of his own life.

As long as he is comparing it to what should have or what he wished would have happened, he is not accepting the experience and not allowing it to truly influence his self-system. As long as this happens, Jamie's self-system is refusing to accept what happened and is holding onto what he wanted to have happen (i.e., his desires). He does this because his self-system cannot deal with the painful experience (his system of maintaining his energy level does not work if that experience is incorporated) and therefore holds on to what his self-system can deal with (what he wanted to have happen) and refuses the painful experience. On the other hand, if he incorporates this experience into his self-system and grows and develops from this, he will no longer need to use his defenses and he will no longer be upset (i.e., feel anxiety) about the experience and he will behave less aggressively (usually there is more than one experience that makes us defensive). This is the process of overcoming painful experiences.

When we cannot integrate an experience into our self-system, we leave it out of our understanding of who we are and how we relate to the world. We separate it from ourselves and leave it outside of our self-system. It is sort of like refusing to let someone into our house. We refuse to let the person influence us. In the same way, we refuse to let an experience influence us. The problem is, we know that the person is outside the door if we are refusing to let him/her in. Because we know that the person is right there, outside of our door, that thought itself influences us in subtle ways. In the same way, we shut out whatever we cannot come to terms with from our consciousness, but it still bothers us because somewhere in our subconscious mind, we know it is there. It bothers us even more when we are reminded of the person outside the door like when our brother says, "why don't you let him in?" In the same way, it may bother Jamie more when he hears voices similar to his father's because he is reminded of something he is trying to shut out. However, when we allow that person inside our house, it breaks down our cozy comfort zone. But eventually, we rebuild it so that we are comfortable with that person inside, just like when we eventually make friends and become comfortable with someone we are initially uncomfortable with. In the same way, when Jamie allows that experience to influence him, it will break down his self-system that he was comfortable with. But eventually, the self-system will be rebuilt with the anxiety inducing experience as part of it. In the beginning, his self-system was refusing to let it in. After he integrates this painful experience as part of his self-system, he no longer has to protect himself from it. He no longer feels the anxiety from it and his shell becomes softer and thinner. The weight has lifted off his shoulders (or out of his shell) and he has more energy (air). Of course, this change does not happen overnight. Jamie has spent many years holding onto his self-system and therefore it will take quite a bit of work for him (perhaps multiple years of effort) to let it go and rebuild a new one.

NEGATIVE EXPERIENCES AND LOSING TOUCH

As we have learned in the previous sections, negative experiences lead to monkeys on our backs. The monkeys on our backs influence our interaction patterns. These monkeys also have another important consequence. They make us tough. They make us build thick shells around us to protect ourselves from future negative experiences. If you can recall the ocean analogy, it is the same thing as closing our pores and becoming defensive (self-protective). We try to protect our air (energy) that we have with all our might so that nobody can dump water on us. We become like this because of negative experiences in the past. We are anxious that it might happen again. Because we fear that it might happen again, we close our pores and build thick shells around us so that nobody and can dump water into us.

Unfortunately, having this thick shell not only prevents having water dumped on us, but also prevents the air and water from spontaneously flowing in and out of our body. In other words, it prevents us from opening up to people and new experiences. The fact that we do not allow water to come inside (as much) represents the idea that we do not attend to other things and other people (as much). We lose respect for and stop paying attention to our surroundings and become insensitive to what goes on in the environment. It prevents us from giving and taking naturally and it prevents us from experiencing unity and identifying with anyone or anything around us. People commonly discuss the desensitization to violence due to the abundance of violence in movies, computer games, and television. It is the same type of thing. It is painful to see someone stabbed or even just verbally offended when we are young because we have not been desensitized from these things yet. But if we are exposed to these incidents of violence (defined by radical taking of energy) many times, we harden our shell (because they are painful experiences) and we no longer identify with the people (or animals or plants or anything) getting hurt and we stop feeling their pain. We don't allow these experiences to influence us anymore. This is how we develop the ability to do very cruel things to other people and things. This is how we stop caring. This is what psychologists mean when they say that someone is losing touch with their true self[26].

In addition, since other people do not influence us as much when we have thick shells, we also stop feeling their joy as well. In fact, when we stop allowing things to influence us, we stop feeling. We only feel when we care. We only feel when we pay attention to things. We only feel when we allow things to influence us. We never feel sad or happy or angry or excited about something we don't care about. We feel because we care. We feel because people and things influence us. Therefore, not feeling is a sign that you have stopped truly interacting with the world (because you are not allowing things to influence you). Not feeling is a sign that you are no longer participating as a member of the universe. Not feeling is a sign that you have withdrawn from life because life, by definition, implies interaction. Not feeling is a sign that you are dead inside. Of course we cannot completely close ourselves off from everything around us just as we cannot completely stop interacting with the environment. But the more we close ourselves off, the less we feel. This implies that negative experiences not only have the tendency to harden our shells but also have the tendency to stop us from feeling.

We all know that negative experiences make us feel numb. If we think of the ocean analogy, we notice that building thick shells not only keeps air and water from flowing in and out of ourselves freely (which represents the idea that we become insensitive to our surroundings), but also decreases the amount of air inside of us. The thick shells take up more space inside of us. The more space our shell takes, the less space we have for air and water inside of us. The less space we have for air and water, the less variability there is in how much water there is inside of us. The less variability there is in the amount of water inside of us, the less variability there is in how good or bad (i.e., energized or de-energized) we feel. In other words, the things that happen to us make less of a difference to us. What this means is that having a hard shell implies not only that we are impervious to things that occur in the environment but also insensitive to our own feelings. Having a hard shell means that we have lost much of our capacity to feel.

The fact that the space that could be used for air inside of us is used for the shell represents that idea that we have lost some capacity to feel. The wall of the shell contains our defenses caused by experiences of fear, anxiety, and feeling of inferiority and inadequacy. The more of these things we have, the thicker our shells become and the thicker our shells, the less variability there is in the amount of air we can have inside (see Figure 14). Furthermore, although we respond indirectly by stealing energy as a reaction to the effects of these things inside our shell (i.e., defenses), we have detached ourselves from and are insensitive to all of those things. This is also why having a hard shell allows us to do extremely cruel things to others.

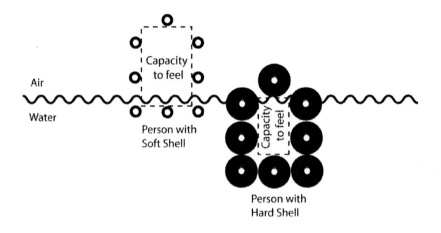

Figure 14. Hard Shells and Losing the Capacity to Feel

For example, a little boy in an abusive home may develop a thick shell to protect himself from being abused in the future but also protects himself mentally by shielding himself from the pain experienced from the abuse. Whenever he is abused, he takes that part of his experience out of his conscious awareness and refuses to let it into his self-system. Because the experience is so painful, he holds on to his desires (e.g., to be loved and cared for) and ignores what is happening (i.e., being abused). This makes the experience less painful for him but at the same time, he loses touch with his own feelings. He may dissociate himself (i.e., self-system) from the painful experience so much that he is no longer aware of anything he is feeling when he is abused. This experience is represented by the person with a thick shell in the ocean analogy in Figure 14. According to the ocean analogy, it is as if this boy places all of his defenses from the painful experience in the shell and makes it very thick. Because his shell is very thick, there is less space inside and this makes for less variability in the amount of air he can have inside. Less variability in the amount of air inside means he has lost much of his capacity to feel. As a result of the abuse, he may not only steal an enormous amount of energy from others (because the thick shells make him sink and water keeps seeping in), but may do so without feeling any guilt or remorse because he has lost the capacity to feel himself. As you can imagine, the extreme version of this is the psychopath (people who do extremely cruel things to others repetitively without any feelings of remorse or guilt).

This is what happens when people commonly say that someone is out of touch with themselves. Because they have shut themselves off from their experiences, they not only have lost much of their ability to interact and grow from their experiences, but they have lost the capacity to feel. In sum, negative experiences have many unwanted consequences. They not only make us scavengers but also makes us self-protective and insensitive to others as well as diminish our own capacity to feel.

As we can see, our life experiences form our self-system. Moreover, the more negative our life experiences, the more closed-minded and defensive our self-system becomes (unless we overcome the negative experiences). In the next sections, we will look at how this theory of the self-system applies to our real life relationships and what we can do about the things that occur in our relationships.

Practical Relationship Applications

Leadership, Parenting, and the Use and Abuse of Social Power

From the sections above, we can understand that it is crucial for individuals in positions of social power to refrain from abusing their power as much as possible. As parents, teachers, caretakers of the elderly, and managers of companies, summer camp leaders, older brothers, coaches etc. we are in positions of social power. As mentioned earlier, social power is nothing more than being able to take more energy than you give. If we abuse this power, we end up doing just that, taking more than we give. Parents sometimes abuse little children but little children cannot abuse their parents. Most of us are in a position of social power in at least some of our relationships. You may be an older sibling, a manager, a scout leader, a coach, a parent, or just a child who is physically bigger than another. As people in social power, we need to be careful not to abuse the power that we have. If we do abuse our power and consistently take energy from people who have less power, we make those less powerful people into scavengers. The more we do this, the more anxious they become, and the worse their scavenging tends to become. This is why parenting is often considered to be a crucial factor in personality development (even though there are many other factors).

As parents, we should not abuse our social power because we create scavengers this way. We create people who live a life of anxiety and try to blame their unhappiness on other people and steal energy from them. This does not mean that parents should become pushovers and not tell children what to do or what not to do. It means that parents (or any other person in power) should respect, listen and pay attention to their children (or anyone less powerful) and attend to their needs as well as guide and direct their behaviors in a respectful manner. As parents, we should demand respect but we should also respect the desires of our children just as much. As managers, we should respect the desires of our workers just as much as they respect us. Real leadership is not abusing one's own power for one's own benefit but organizing people to function effectively together without anyone stealing excessive amounts of energy from anyone else. Even though people who are in positions of social power are often tempted to abuse their power for their own benefit, it is extremely important to resist that temptation. Resisting that temptation is not only beneficial to other people or society in general but to our selves in the long run as well. If we look at the history of humankind, we can easily learn that nothing good results from the abuse of power. This abuse of social power may provide temporary relief or joy (because we feel energized), but almost always leads to something much worse in the long run.

Resisting our own temptations that make us abuse our power and trying to stop stealing energy is easier said than done. We all have our anxieties. We are all anxious of certain things and people that may steal our energy because they have in the past. Nobody has had a perfect life. We all have had painful experiences and we all use defenses. And because we have these defenses, we all have developed patterns of stealing energy. Even though some do more than others, everybody scavenges to a certain extent. Yes, that includes you and me. We are all tempted at times to abuse our own power. We may not be consciously aware of the fact that we do abuse our power, or that we steal energy at all. We may not even be aware that we are tempted to do so. But we all do.

How can we avoid abusing our power and avoid stealing energy from others if we carry all of these scars that makes us afraid of losing energy? We ourselves want to load up on energy to prepare for events that deplete our own energy tank. The only way to get over this anxiety is to first become aware of the defenses we use and become aware of our tendencies of stealing energy in response to anxiety. Then we must examine our desires that we are holding onto that are preventing us from accepting and integrating our painful experiences into our self-system. Once we learn which desires we are holding onto, we must try to let them go. As we have seen, although stealing energy may drive us toward positive experiences in the short run (by increasing one's energy level temporarily), it almost always leads to much more negative experiences in the long run. It makes scavengers out of others and none of us want to live in a world full of scavengers. Of course, this change does not happen overnight. We have spent years repressing or denying the painful experiences and years using these habits of stealing energy and therefore it will take quite a bit of work for us to unlearn them. Letting go of our desires is a lot easier said than done. It takes time and we must be patient with ourselves when we go through the process and we must be even more patient with others when they go through the process.

DEALING WITH ENERGY THIEVES

While we are discussing the realistic aspects of all of this, let's focus on another realistic problem that we encounter quite often in our lives. What do we do when someone is stealing energy from us? We have all been in situations like this and sometimes we wonder what we can do about it. There are no quick fixes for this problem but there may be a few things worth noting in order to increase your chances of changing the situation into a relatively positive experience. Usually, our natural reaction to this type of situation is not the wisest. When people steal energy from us, we experience emotional hijacking and respond with the fight or flight response. Let's examine these two natural responses.

The first natural reaction we commonly have when someone steals our energy is to become anxious and steal energy right back (i.e., the fight response). However, from what we have learned until now, we know that this is the last thing we should do. When we steal energy back from someone stealing energy from us, we induce more anxiety in the other person and motivate him/her even more to steal energy from us. And if they cannot steal energy from us, they will find someone or something else to steal energy from and that is not what we want either. We must remember that the other person is stealing energy from us because s/he feels low in energy to begin with (thus is motivated to replenish his/her energy). When we steal energy back from people stealing energy from us, they start losing energy again and become afraid of running out of energy. They then will be motivated to replenish their energy even more and since we are the ones they are interacting with, we are their prime targets for stealing energy. Thus, stealing energy back is not really the answer to this problem even though it may be temporarily effective.

The other possible natural reaction we have when someone steals energy from us is to escape and avoid the other person so that they cannot continue to steal energy from us. This maybe a reasonable response that may benefit us personally in the short run if we no longer intend to continue a relationship with that other person. However, in many cases, we do continue relationships with people who steal energy from us. These people are often important people to us, such as our spouse, our parents, our children, our siblings, our co-workers, our best friends etc. and we neither want to avoid those people for the rest of our lives nor escape from them every time they steal our energy. We want to develop a positive relationship with them and if we keep avoiding them, we will never be able to do that.

In any case, the natural reaction is defensiveness of some form. We either take energy back or we escape the situation. Although these reactions may be very helpful when we are in a life or death situation, most of these types of situations are not life or death type situations. So what should we do? There are two things we should keep in mind. One is to avoid defensiveness of any form as much as possible. When we are defensive, we tune out and shut the other person out. We refuse to allow them to influence us. This is what happens when we steal energy back and this is also what happens when we avoid someone. The key is to do the exact opposite, "open up and allow the other person in". Let them influence you and learn to adapt to their influence. As mentioned earlier, this can be done if we let go of our own desires. The key thing to remember is that we only experience interpersonal conflict when our desires do not match the desires of others. Therefore, if we let go of our own desires, we can naturally accept the other person's desires and allow them to influence us.

The other thing to keep in mind is to do what you would want the other person to do if you were in the other person's shoes. We often hear the expression "Lead by example". This usually means don't tell people what to do or how to do things. Just do it the way it you think it should be done. If it is actually a very good way to do it, people will learn just by observing your behavior and its consequences. They may not pick it up right away, but eventually, if you are very patient with them, they will pick it up. Whenever people are ready to learn from your leadership, they will. We need to be very patient, however, because people need to be at a certain psychological stage in their lives to learn particular things. If they are not at the right stage, they won't get it no matter how hard you try. It takes time to heal from painful experiences. We often cannot let go of our defenses overnight. We often cannot let go of our desires overnight. It may take multiple years in some cases. Some people are able to let go faster than others and others may take a lifetime to let go. We just need to be patient.

Why should we refrain from telling others what to do and how to do things? When we tell others what to do or how to do things, we are essentially taking energy from them. No matter how you say it, the underlying message is "I want you to respect my way even though I don't respect your way" and that is exactly what taking energy (or stealing energy if it is done in an extreme way) is about. And as mentioned earlier, if we steal energy, we motivate the other to steal energy back from us.

How can we stay calm and not become emotionally hijacked when someone steals energy from us. This is another thing that is much easily said than done but remember that there are two ways of replenishing our energy. One is by taking from the environment and the other is experiencing unity with the environment. When we feel like we are losing energy, it is because we feel that only the air in our body is our energy, we have forgotten that all of the air around us is our energy. If we remind ourselves that all of the air around us is our energy and directly experience this at a deep emotional level, we do not have to steal energy because we are already replenished. This is not the same thing as just cognitively telling yourself that all of the air around you is your energy. It involves an experiential and emotional change (i.e., we have to feel it from the heart). Not only do we have to think differently, we also must feel differently from this adjustment. It involves truly letting go of our desires and not just saying that we have let them go. We have to not only experience this in our mind but also experience this with our heart and our whole being. This is when we are really replenished and feel full of energy.

If on the other hand, we feel emotionally hijacked already, we need to take a time out until our hormones in our body subside. As mentioned earlier, this takes at least 30 minutes if not more (depending on how upset we are and how long we are dwelling on the problem while we are taking our time out). It does seem awkward to take a time out in the middle of a conversation or an argument but if you do not take it, you go into battle in full force. And although going into battle in full force has its own merits, as we will see later, the process itself is not very pleasant. Therefore, if there is an alternative that is equally or more effective (like taking a time out), it may be useful to use it.

The whole idea among transpersonal psychologists is that the completely transcendent person never needs to steal energy because all of the air around them is their air. This type of person is never anxious (i.e., never afraid of anything) and never needs to close his or her pores. This helps them stay above water and makes them unafraid of giving energy away (i.e., having water dumped into them). They are not even afraid of death if they are experiencing complete transcendence. This is the goal according to the transpersonal view discussed in many of the eastern traditions such as Buddhism, Hinduism as well as modern Western writers such as Allan Watts and Ken Wilber[27]. Although this may be too idealistic for most of us (including myself), this is what we can try to be like as much as possible. In trying to become more like this, we experience states slightly closer to the state of complete transcendence.

SETTING BOUNDARIES

Realistically speaking, most of us are not experiencing states that are even close to transcendence most of the time. Therefore, most of us cannot help but feel depleted of energy sometimes in our lives. Some people may feel depleted more than others but it is only the rare person who experiences satori or nirvana (other common terms in Buddhism, and Hinduism respectively, for complete transcendence) that never feels depleted. Most of us are afraid of losing energy, losing the air (in the ocean analogy), losing respect, losing important people around us, losing our own lives etc. At some moments, we may be more anxious and afraid of these things than others but the point is that most of us do not live in complete transcendence. So for the rest of us mere mortals who value life more than death and thus like having lots of energy more than very little energy, the question is, "Is there any other constructive way to deal with people stealing energy from us when we are not strong enough to open our pores and let the water flow freely in and out of us?"

In the literature on psychotherapy, people often use the term "setting boundaries"[28]. In "energy" language, this refers to our behavior stating, "You can only take this much energy from me. If you take more than that, I will start taking back from you." We intuitively do this to each other so that the other person knows when to stop teasing a friend, when to stop nagging at someone, or when to stop joking around. The people send us signals (often non-verbal) telling us to back off at a certain point. In this way, we (subconsciously in most cases) negotiate how much energy we can take and in what ways we can take energy from others in our relationships. Although this is mostly done at a subconscious level we can also do this consciously if someone is stealing energy from us and we are not strong enough to become or remain transcendent. We can politely send signals to the person that this behavior may no longer be tolerated (either verbally or non-verbally). In a conversation, we may state that we respect how the other person feels but we are not ready to discuss this issue now and state this directly in a non-aggressive, non-threatening way. We must be honest with ourselves and with others by noticing and admitting that we are afraid of losing more energy (e.g., "Sorry, I know this is important to you but it is too painful for me to talk about this now." or "Sorry, I understand that you feel strongly about this but I am not strong enough to face this yet."). When we do this, we make ourselves vulnerable by opening up and expressing our pain and anxieties but if we are dealing with an important relationship that we wish to improve, it may be a risk worth taking. In lighter cases of others taking energy from us, (i.e., the other person is not too motivated to steal energy from us even though s/he is doing it), it may be enough to gently change the topic of conversation to something safer, minimize your response indicating non-verbally that you don't want to go there, or just directly asking them to stop the behavior.

In this way, we are gently taking a little bit of energy back from the other person and sending a subtle warning saying, "You are about to cross the line. Please respect it." In other words, you are saying, "I'm starting to care less about your desires to replenish your energy and care more about my desires. Now, I want you to respect my boundaries (i.e., desires)." If these signs are ignored, and the other person keeps stealing energy from us, it may be best to politely leave the other person and escape from the situation or take a time-out before we reengage.

If the other person is someone very close to us that we do not want to leave, then we must re-examine our relationship with him/her and work on it together with that person. This may take considerable effort and time. If we do not want to leave that person, we are most likely dependent on him/her to take energy from as well. In this case, both parties need to examine themselves and develop more self-awareness of their defenses and their tendencies to take energy from the other. This is often a painful and difficult process but it will be extremely rewarding once it is accomplished to a certain extent. We may have to face things about ourselves that we have been denying and repressing. We may fight with each other about the patterns of stealing energy we have. The relationship may be extremely rocky at certain times during this process. In the end, we usually feel that it was worth it.

During this process, we will also need to develop an understanding of how the other person perceives things to develop shared consciousness. We must agree on what behaviors are interpreted as taking energy and what behaviors are interpreted as giving energy. In sum, we will need to develop more self-awareness and develop respect and understanding of both the desires of ourselves and those of the other person by engaging in self-examination and communication.

In sum, when we are not strong enough to stay transcendent, it may sometimes be useful to take a little energy back and send signals about one's own boundaries (I am getting close to my limit. You are about to cross the line. I don't want you to do this. Please step back). This is what the T.V. hero does when s/he is trying to convince the dangerous person to put his/her weapon down and come to peace with him/herself or someone else. The hero provides the other person an opportunity to gently step back and let go of their behavior pattern without making them too defensive and motivating them to take energy back (or keep stealing energy). It is important only to take a little bit of energy back instead of stealing large amounts of energy from the other person. If we burst in anger or criticize or use any extreme method of stealing energy in response to this, we make the other person feel depleted of energy and motivate them to replenish their energy by stealing back again and the cycle may keep repeating itself. Even though we are trying to kill the fire, we are, in essence, feeding the fire and this is the last thing we want to do in this situation.

It is important also to note that, although this may be a realistic alternative for us mere mortals when faced with such a situation (i.e., when others steal energy from us), people taking a completely transpersonal perspective would never recommend this. This is because, to reach the state of transcendence, we must let go of all of our desires and defenses and overcome this illusion of believing that the self is only this stuff inside our bag of skin and overcome our anxiety of losing energy. And if we never overcome this illusion/anxiety, we will never reach the state of complete transcendence.

Even though transcendence is the ultimate goal, we must understand the process of approaching this goal. One way we can look at this process is by examining how our interpersonal relationships develop. Through the insights of various theorists, I have developed a framework consisting of four stages in the development of interpersonal relationships. The next section will discuss the four stages in chronological order.

FOUR STAGES OF RELATIONSHIPS

Considering the things that have been discussed so far, there seem to be four general stages that we go through whenever we develop a relationship. The transition between the stages may be more gradual than a progression of separate stages but it may be easier to explain them in separate blocks (i.e., stages). These stages apply to a variety of relationships such as close friendships, romantic relationships, work relationships, and even parent-child relationships to some extent. It may also be important to note that even though they will be explained primarily in the context of a two-person relationship, this applies to relationships among more individuals as well (although the more people involved, the more complex it becomes). It may also be applied to situations where two or more groups (instead of individuals) form and develop relationships.

1. Mutual interest stage

The first stage characterizes the very beginning of a relationship. For a relationship to develop, both individuals must be interested in forming a relationship with the other. In order to form a relationship with the other, both individuals must be interested, accepting, and respecting of the other to a certain extent. Each party must attend to the other's desires to a certain extent. In other words, each must provide the other with some energy. Nobody wants to form a relationship with anyone who is not respectful of us in any way. Nobody wants to form a relationship with a person who does not attend to our desires at all. When both individuals are interested in forming a relationship and receive energy from each other to some extent, we have a beginning of a relationship. This is how all relationships begin. We do not know each other well in the beginning and so we are interested in each other, we pay attention to each other and we are respectful of each other. Everything about the other person seems new and interesting. We feel good and energized during this stage and this motivates us further to maintain and pursue the relationship. We often feel energized during this stage because we commonly experience unity, a sense of togetherness with each other. According to the ocean analogy, we feel like we share the air inside of us. We respect and attend to each other's desires very much and this makes us feel a sense of unity with each other.

In most cases, it is clear that a relationship develops because both parties are interested in developing the relationship but some may say that sometimes, people are forced into relationships. Even if one party feels forced to be in the relationship, there is always something to be gained on both sides. Relationships only exist if there is something to be gained by both parties. In some extreme cases, a person may gain energy just from the fact that s/he is able to stay alive if s/he maintains the relationship. That person is still choosing to stay in the relationship and thus perhaps choosing to stay alive as well. It is still their choice and they are still gaining something from it.

This applies to all types of relationships including romantic relationships. It refers to the "Falling in Love" phase in the beginning of a romantic relationship. Although, the emotional impact of this stage is much more pronounced in romantic relationships because various additional hormones and social expectations are involved, the underlying dynamics is still the same. Both individuals are interested in forming the relationship and both respect each other and attend to each other's desires. There is mutual respect and mutual attention and thus we experience unity, a sense of togetherness with each other.

2. Power struggle stage

After a while, both individuals get to know each other very well and begin paying less attention to each other. Even though we are now committed to the relationship to a certain extent, the novelty wears off (and the spark in the relationship is gone) and the other person is not as interesting as before. We begin paying less and less attention to each other, and we begin respecting each other less and less. The honeymoon is over. We stop appreciating the other person's existence and we start getting annoyed at the little things they do. We begin taking each other for granted and begin trying to use the other person for one's own personal benefit. We begin wanting to change the other person into what we want them to be like regardless of what the other person wants. This happens with romantic couples, roommates, friends, coworkers, anyone that we have known for a while. In other words, we begin trying to take more energy than we give to the other person. At this stage, we know that we are committed to each other to a certain extent and take each other for granted.

When we are in this stage, we often find ourselves having arguments and fights trying to decide who is more powerful or who is right. Do I attend to your desires or do you attend to my desires. Regardless of what you argue about, the underlying message is the same. "You attend to my desires!" "No, you attend to my desires!" Each individual wants to be the most powerful one in the relationship so that they can have their desires attended to most of the time. But of course if you are the most powerful, someone else has to be less powerful and nobody wants to be the less powerful one who is not attended to. This is why we tend to fight and argue often in this stage. We are essentially fighting for social power. In a parent-child relationship this is when the child goes through the anal stage of development (around 2 years of age). Both the parent and the child begin differentiating themselves from each other and both parties try to control the other.

At the same time we are fighting and arguing for power, we are also negotiating how (and how much) you can take energy from each other. We are trying to see what works. The underlying dialogue in the arguments is not only that each person wants power, but there is also a negotiation taking place. We are both trying to find out how (and how much) the other person allows us to take his/her energy. We are, in a sense, testing each other out. We want to know how much we can get away with. We discussed different methods of stealing energy earlier (see the section on The Stealing of Energy). In this stage, we are trying various methods out (in many cases we start out with the methods that have been successful in our past relationships) to see what the other person will allow (and in what circumstances they are allowed). It is largely a process of trial and error. I may find out that this other person does not allow me to steal energy from her by intimidating her but will allow me to steal lots of energy by interrogating and criticizing her. I may also find out that, in certain circumstances, she will allow me to take some energy from her by being aloof. At the same time, the other person may find out that I allow her to steal large amounts of energy from me by being aloof and charismatic but only allow her to take a tiny bit of energy from me by chainchatting or interrogation. In this way we figure out ways to take energy from each other and sub-consciously try to arrive at an agreement about how (and how much) we allow each other to steal energy from the other. Once we come to an agreement, we settle into the relationship even more until at least one person in the relationship wants to change the terms. If this happens, there is usually a negotiation period often accompanied with lots of arguments and fighting again until both arrive at a new agreement.

When two people keep interacting with each other even though they seem to dislike each other, they are in the power struggle stage. In this case, both still want to have a relationship with the other. Both individuals cannot leave the other alone because both want to show the other that he or she is the more powerful one and is therefore in control of the relationship. They are striving to come to an agreement about who is more powerful and how each person will allow the other to take energy from them. When they come to an agreement on this, the power struggle is over.

The power struggle stage is the stage we are often in when two or more groups of individuals fight with one another. Each group wants a relationship with the other group but wants to be the more powerful one. An extreme example of this is war. All fights between two or more parties, whether they are individuals or groups, are power struggles and it is part of the process of relationship development. And from our experiences, we notice that some power struggles are more dangerous and hurtful than others. The point is not to eliminate the power struggle (because that would mean eliminating the relationship) but to engage in the power struggle in smooth and constructive manner as possible.

In many cases, the relationship may come to an end if the parties do not come to an agreement and lose motivation to maintain the relationship because they are tired of negotiating. In fact, when relationships end, they typically tend to come to an end during this stage. When both parties cannot agree on what they allow and what they will not allow (methods and amount of giving and taking energy) and they lose motivation to continue negotiating, both parties distance themselves from each other so that they have minimal interaction with each other. In a marital relationship, this is typically when people file for divorce.

3. Codependence stage

As mentioned earlier, when two parties come to an agreement about how and how much energy can be taken from each other, they settle into the relationship even more. Even though we are not consciously aware of this in most of our relationships, each party knows how much energy they can take from the other, and how (and in what circumstances) they are allowed to take energy from the other. The rules of the game are established and now the game is played over and over. At this stage of the relationship, a routine is established and we repeat our interpersonal patterns of taking energy from each other over and over. I take in certain ways and then you take in certain other ways and we are both fine with that. If we use the ocean analogy, it means that we both have a habit of pouring water on each other (see Figure 15).

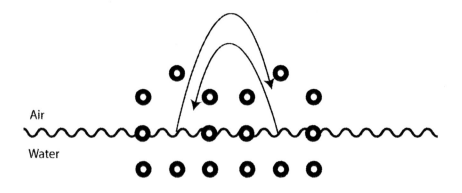

Figure 15. Codependence

Even though we may not be completely satisfied with the relationship, if we reach this stage, we have settled for what we have to a certain extent. We become used to this type of interaction and we begin to expect it out of each other. And because it is expected, we feel uncomfortable if it does not happen. Therefore, we not only expect the other person to take our energy in a certain way but we begin to desire it. In a sense, there is a certain amount of unity between the two people in the codependence stage, because both individuals are behaving according to what the other person desires.

It is important to remember, however, that this is a simplified model of what really happens. There is no clear-cut line that divides the power struggle stage and the codependence stage. The difference between the power struggle stage and the codependence stage is relative. The cycle of giving and taking energy from each other does not repeat in exactly the same way all of the time. Even though both parties have settled on the basic rules, there is still a continuous negotiation of the rules at a smaller level. The negotiation may not be as heated as in the power struggle stage, but things happen in life, circumstances change, and we try out different things to see if we can change the rules for our benefit. The main part of the negotiation, however, is over at this stage.

4. Deep mutual respect stage

After spending considerable time in the codependence stage, some of our relationships gradually change in a positive way. Little by little, we begin letting go of our desires that make us defensive and steal energy. We begin to worry less about running out of energy. We begin realizing through our experiences that things are smoother if we just let go of our desires and worry less about running out of energy. And because we worry less about running out of energy, we feel much less motivated to steal energy from the other. And because we are less motivated to steal energy from the other (i.e., we are emotionally stable), our relationships become much smoother. We stop stealing energy from each other and respect and attend to each other more.

You may remember from earlier sections that we can energize ourselves in one of two ways. One is by taking energy from other people and things. The other way is by experiencing unity with the environment such as other people. During the power struggle and the codependence stage, we have been trying to energize ourselves primarily by taking energy from the other person. When we gradually move toward the stage of mutual respect, we are intuitively realizing that it is better to energize ourselves by experiencing unity through mutual respect and attention rather than taking energy from each other.

This move toward deeper mutual respect is a gradual process. There is no clear-cut line that divides the codependence stage and the stage characterized as deep mutual respect. It is a process of gradually taking less energy from each other and respecting each other more (and attending to the desires of the other person more). It is a process of becoming sensitive, understanding, and forgiving toward each other (since forgiving is the same as letting go of our desires). It is a process of gradually letting go of our desires that cause anxiety. It is a process of gradually experiencing more and more unity and harmony in our relationship. It is a process of moving from the center to the right side of the diagram in Figure 3. This process of experiencing deeper mutual respect with each other is a continuous process. There is no endpoint to this process. We can always experience deeper and deeper mutual respect and attend to each other more. The deeper our mutual respect becomes, the more energizing and gratifying our relationship becomes.

As we can see from the explanation above, we move from stability to instability and then gradually move back towards stability until we are even more stable than the state we started out with. It is important to note that not all relationships go through all four stages. Some relationships disintegrate halfway through the process, some remain in the power struggle or codependence stage until the end of the relationship.

It may also be worthwhile to repeat what was mentioned at the beginning of this section. The progression of stages is a gradual process and there are no clear-cut lines that divide one stage from another. Furthermore, although the stages were explained primarily in the context of a two-person relationship, this applies to relationships among more individuals as well. It may also be applied to situations where two or more groups (instead of individuals) form and develop relationships.

THE PITFALLS OF INTERPERSONAL AND GROUP UNITY

Although all of the previous sections have discussed unity as a positive state of mind, both interpersonal and group unity has its pitfalls. The base of the problem is that, almost all cases of interpersonal and group unity involve the exclusion of someone or something else. If you draw a circle that includes everyone you are in unity with inside of it, there is always someone and something outside of it. In other words, when we experience unity with someone that we have not experienced unity with before, we dissolve the boundary between you and that someone but by doing so, we create a new boundary outside of you and that other person. In most cases, experiencing unity is just the act of moving one's boundaries further out so that the self-system seems more inclusive. This is not really a problem in itself. In fact, as will be discussed in a later section, it is something that just happens as a course of human development in general.

The problem begins in the cases where these boundaries (or shells) outside our self and the people we are in unity with become so hard and thick that it prevents most things from outside that boundary to influence us. When this happens, we become unaccepting of people outside our boundaries and we are unaccepting of ideas that come from outside our boundaries. Fascist societies and cults are prime examples of large groups with this type of characteristic. They have an extreme sense of unity and try to eradicate or ignore anyone who does not fit within their boundaries (or any ideas that do not fit). This can happen in smaller groups such as families, political groups, business groups, friends as well as groups of just two people[29]. Any situation where people feel a strong sense of unity with each other to the extent that they try to eradicate or ignore anyone who does not fit within those boundaries (or any ideas that do not fit) is problematic. When this happens, we become narrow minded and only accept what is inside our boundaries. This is analogous to the individual with hard shells and closed pores that does not allow anything outside of their individual self to influence him or her. Instead of this being just one individual, it is now a group of individuals.

Therefore, when we experience a sense of unity with a certain person or groups of people, it is always useful to be careful not become too narrow minded and disrespectful of others who do not fit in the group. Although this is much easier said than done, this is especially important to keep in mind to avoid extreme types of social conflict because this is the source of all social conflict whether it is group conflict among relatives or war between two nations. The diagrams in Figure 16 illustrate the relative differences between healthy and unhealthy group (or interpersonal) unity.

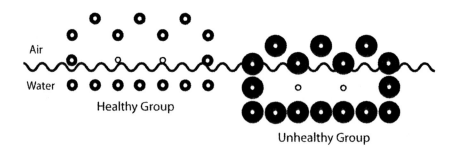

Figure 16. Healthy and Unhealthy Groups

Even though extreme levels of disrespect and ignoring others can be highly problematic, we all understand from our own experiences that when we fight, we fight for a reason. In other words, fighting can sometimes be a very useful experience. This is exactly what happens in the power struggle stage discussed in the previous section. To examine this further, the next section will discuss the significance of fighting in relationships.

THE SIGNIFICANCE OF FIGHTS

As you may have realized from the previous sections, fighting and arguing is not a completely negative thing even if it feels terrible when we are immersed in the process. Most fighting is a negotiation process. By fighting, we negotiate the ways we take energy from others and the ways we allow others to take energy from us. By fighting and arguing, we set our boundaries indicating how and how much energy each person can take from each other. We often fight and argue because we cannot agree on the rules of our relationship. In many cases, people are insecure, scared and become greedy and self-protective. Both parties commonly want as much as possible and usually, that means they want to take more than they give. This is why we commonly fight when we are making the rules for the relationship. The more insecure and scared the individuals in the relationship are, the more fighting there is. But it is important to keep in mind that, this is just part of the process and it will not last forever as long as we learn from these experiences.

In a sense, fighting and arguing is an opportunity to learn about the other person and one's relationship with the other person. This often happens in the earlier stages of the relationship (Power struggle stage) and also when one party decides to change the rules that were established before because they no longer like those rules for some reason (e.g., a person changes jobs and habitually loses more energy at work than before). When one party decides to change the rules, we have to renegotiate the rules and this renegotiation may involve some fighting and arguing (i.e., a rough interaction) again.

Sooner or later, if we are patient enough, we reach an agreement and the relationship will become smoother in most cases. This agreement may be the same as the agreement before we had the fight or it may be different. But even if the agreement ends up being the same as before the fight, we have still feel that we tried and we still have learned that it was not worth changing at this time. This negotiation process may take a few hours or it may take thirty years, just as some conflicts are resolved faster than others. Of course, we sometimes choose not to be patient and give up on the relationship before we come to an agreement. That is our choice. We can try to stick it out or we can let go and move on to another relationship. Either way, you are stuck with both the positive and negative consequences of your choice.

We all know that some relationships last very long and others do not last as long. This is one of the factors that influences how long a relationship lasts. Another important factor relating to how long a relationship will last is compatibility. Some people say, "Birds of a feather flock together." Others say, "Opposites attract." What kinds of factors influence whether a person is compatible with another? This is what the next section is about.

DIFFERENT DANCES AND COMPATIBILITY

Some people have soft thin shells and open pores while others have thick hard shells and relatively close pores. Although we all know that we are more vulnerable when we have softer shells, people with softer shells also have more potential to become emotionally stable. If you have a soft thin shell, you tend to feel comfortable dancing to a very sensitive smooth rhythm of giving and receiving. If you have a thick hard shell you need more stimulation to feel engaged and to get your rhythm going. This is why many people with hard shells enjoy more excitement and are more anxious in general. The harder your shell, the more comfortable you are dancing to a rough rhythm of giving and taking.

Although this may be contradictory to the idea stating that the rougher the rhythm, the more unstable things are, there is a way to explain this. Unstable does not necessarily mean uncomfortable. The people who like more excitement tend to have a hard shell already due to their past experiences. When they interact with other people with a rough rhythm in a rough manner, they feel a sense of comfort because they are familiar with this type of rhythm of giving and taking energy. A person with a relatively hard shell and closed pores has a habit of having others pour large amounts of water into them (i.e., take lots of energy from them). This is why they have a hard shell. As a reaction, this person is also used to taking large amounts of water and pouring it into someone else (i.e., taking lots of energy from others). As we all know, there is comfort in familiarity. In other words, their rhythm is in sync with the rhythm of their immediate environment (the interaction with the other person in this case). In this way, they feel comfortable in a rough interaction with the other person because it is familiar to them. Even though the person is experiencing a rough rhythm interpersonally, they feel a sense of comfort due to the familiarity of the situation. An example of this would be two friends jokingly making sarcastic remarks at each other. They feel comfortable losing relatively large amounts of energy (hearing sarcastic remarks about them) because they feel that they can take back the same amount right afterwards again (by making sarcastic remarks at them). These individuals may be enjoying each other's company and feeling comfortable in this situation even though they may not be experiencing a very deep sense of unity with each other.

This whole idea makes even more sense if we look at this from the point of my desires vs. what has, is, or might happen. If I am used to having people make seemingly hurtful and sarcastic remarks at me, I may get to the point where I desire this. I may feel that people making these remarks at me is better than people not attending to me at all. Thus, even though it may look like the other person is being hurtful towards me, it may be exactly what I desire. In contrast, the other person may also be similar to me and may desire having sarcastic remarks made toward him/her. When this happens and we are both making seemingly hurtful sarcastic remarks at each other, we are actually attending to each other's desires. Because we are attending to each other's desires, we feel a certain amount of unity with each other even though it seems like we are being disrespectful toward each other on the surface.

Lets look at another example. If this same person with a hard shell interacts with a person with a soft shell, this person may feel bored, alienated, and uncomfortable because they are not used to this lack of stimulation or activity. This is because even though they may take large amounts of energy from the other person, the other person with the soft shell does not react by taking large amounts of energy back. Because this person with a hard shell is familiar with and desires situations where others take lots of energy, s/he expects the other to take lots of energy from him or her. The other person with a soft shell does not respond according to his/her expectations and desires and thus places him/her in an unfamiliar (and therefore slightly uncomfortable) situation. In a sense the person with a soft shell is not attending to the desires of the person with a hard shell. The person with the hard shell cannot get the rhythm that they are familiar with going and thus feels out of sync with the environment. On the other hand, the person with a soft shell feels overstimulated and is shaken out of their stable comfort zone when the person with a hard shell takes large amounts of energy from him/her. The soft shelled person does not desire this and therefore the person with the hard shell is perceived as not attending to the his/her desires. They simply do not understand each other's desires. In this case, both individuals feel somewhat uncomfortable since the other person is responding in an unfamiliar and undesirable way to each other and neither of them can be in sync with the other person's rhythm.

It seems like people who have a soft shell feel comfortable interacting with others who have a soft shell in a smooth manner and people who have a hard shell like interacting with people who have a hard shell in a rough manner. Interacting with people that match our own rhythm, enables us to experience unity because the other person seems to attend to our desires (i.e., expectations). This makes sense because a relationship does not work well if one person takes more energy than the other. From the perspective of interpersonal behavior patterns discussed earlier, people who match our own rhythms have interpersonal behavior patterns that are compatible with us. If I have a pattern of stealing large amounts of energy from others, people who have a pattern of stealing large amounts of energy back from me may feel more comfortable with me than people who have a pattern of only taking small amounts of energy from others.

This may also be the reason why some people like loud and harsh sounding music and shocking art while others like quiet, harmonious, and calming types of music and art. Loud and harsh sounding music and shocking art demands a lot of attention and thus takes lots of energy from us. Because people with a hard shell are familiar with things that take large amounts of energy from us, they are attracted to these things. In contrast, quiet, harmonious, and calming types of music and art demand less attention and thus take less energy from us and allow us to experience more harmony, unity and togetherness. Because people with a soft shell are more familiar with harmony, unity, and togetherness as well as things that only take small amounts of energy from us, they are attracted to these things. In sum, we are attracted to not only people but also various objects and sensory experiences that are compatible to our own rhythm.

In a sense, we like what we are familiar with. If we are used to a rough rhythm, we want (i.e., desire) our environment to be rough to us. If the environment is rough to us, we feel unity because what happens matches our desires even if it seems like it is unstable from the outside. This is why some people are not bothered by yelling at each other all day. It is what they are used to and it is what they desire. If we are used to a smooth rhythm, we may like interacting with the world in a smooth manner. Lastly, although we may be comfortable with people who have similar size pores and similar size shells, deep unity through mutual respect and harmony requires not only a match in shell and pore size but also a smooth interpersonal rhythm between the individuals. This is experienced more as a calm, spiritual sense of unity.

When we develop relationships with other people, we not only want to feel energized and have a good time with them but we also want to help each other grow. However, as many of us know from our own experiences, helping each other grow is a task that is much easier said than done. Let's examine the concept of growth and maturation in the context of interpersonal relationships.

DEVELOPMENTAL READINESS AND OUR NATURAL MOTIVATION TO GROW

Sometimes in our relationships, we want others to see things in our own way just for very selfish reasons (i.e., just to steal energy). At other times, we want them to see things in our way because we truly believe that it will help them grow and develop. However, I have learned that people need to be at a certain psychological stage in their lives to learn particular things. Even if something seems obvious to you, it does not necessarily mean that someone else can understand it right away if you explain it well. If we are not at the right stage in life, we won't understand certain things no matter how hard we try. We all know that we cannot teach calculus to a two year-old child because the child is not at the developmental stage for that yet. In the same way, we only learn certain things in life when we are ready for it.

There are several possible reasons for this. One simple reason is that we can only pay attention to a certain amount of things at any time. Thus we can only learn things at a certain rate. Another reason may be more technical. In order for integrations to take place, the differentiation of the elements to be integrated must have taken place. If you want to learn about complementary colors, you need to know what colors are in the first place. If you want to learn algebra, you need to know what numbers are in the first place. Another reason may be that the very act of trying to get people to learn something that you want them to learn invites resistance. It is an act of taking (or stealing) energy and thus invites the response of the other person to take energy back or becoming defensive at the very least. As the proverb of the Lakota native tribe translates "Force, no matter how concealed, begets resistance".

The final and perhaps most important reason is that sometimes we build shells that are too thick to allow anything meaningful to affect us. This is what happens when we experience traumatic (or merely painful) experiences. We build a thick shell and do not allow anything to affect us. When we do not allow things to affect us, we do not grow. In other words, we must allow others to take our energy if we want to grow. The thicker our shells are, the less others are able to dump water on us. This implies that the thicker our shells, the less prepared we are to learn anything new. It takes time for people to overcome painful experiences. We need time to heal and let go of our desires. We need time to allow their shells to soften again. When people have thick shells, we sometimes must wait until they let go of their desires (i.e., what we want or what should/ought to happen). We must wait until they can let their guard down and allow new information to enter again.

When we cannot deal with a painful experience, we use defenses and make our shells thicker to protect ourselves from it. The more painful the experience, the thicker and harder we make our shells to protect ourselves from it. A person can only learn when s/he softens his/her shell. We can help them, but we have to be patient and wait for them to meet us halfway. We can do things to facilitate the softening of other people's shells but ultimately, only the person him or herself can soften his or her own shells. In some cases, this may take a few minutes and in other cases, this may take many years.

We all have a natural motivation to grow and develop. The problem is that sometimes we are hurt so much that we lose touch with that motivation to grow. The more painful experiences we have not come to terms with, the harder our shells become. And the harder our shells become, the more we lose touch with our motivation to grow. However, although people who have become defensive and have developed thicker shells may be less motivated to learn and grow than people who are less defensive and have softer shells, we are all born with a natural motivation to learn, grow, and constantly adapt to the changing environment. And though people will not learn things until they are ready, in many cases, they will learn naturally when they are ready regardless of whether we ourselves help them learn or not. In many cases, people learn similar lessons from their own experiences or from someone else even if we are not the ones who help them learn. This does not imply that helping others to learn is a useless endeavor. It is in many cases a very fruitful endeavor. However, having this perspective helps us become more hopeful and patient when we are trying to help others learn (since we think that even if we are temporarily unsuccessful in helping them, they will learn when the time comes). In sum, two factors; being at the right stage, and being in touch with our natural motivation to learn are perhaps the most important keys to meaningful learning. From an interpersonal standpoint, this implies that not only must we be patient with other people, but we must also have faith that people will learn what they need to learn when they are ready for it.

Despite the fact that people will not learn certain things unless they are at the right stage of development, people do try to force others to learn things and sometimes it is very effective. However, their stage of life in most cases is roughly accounted for even when people are successful using the forceful way. The next section explores how these forceful methods sometimes work.

THE DIFFICULTIES OF FORCING OTHERS TO GROW

There are generally two schools of thought concerning how to help other people develop. One is the forceful way and the other is the patient way. Let us examine the forceful way first. The forceful way implies that in order for people to change, they need to be rattled out of the comfort zone of their self-system. People need to be rattled out of the patterns they feel comfortable with. The reason they are comfortable with it is because they know from past experience that they are safe as long as they stay within those patterns (in their self-system). This is why familiarity is so comforting to us. The problem with this is that sometimes we try so hard to maintain our patterns to the extent that we resist anything that makes us change these patterns (even if it is for positive change). In order to change these patterns, we need to rattle these people out of these patterns so that they will change. What we essentially do if we take this approach is we make it so that the patterns they are comfortable with no longer work. We do things so that their familiar patterns are no longer safe. We may design things so that these patterns lead to aversive consequences. This naturally forces individuals to change their patterns because the patterns they we using no longer work. Basically, we create a problem for the individual and force the individual to deal with the problem.

This method works as long as the individual conceptualizes the problem as his/her own problem rather than a problem of the outside world. If the person conceptualizes this as a problem in the outside world, the person does not change his/her patterns. He/she simply manipulates things and people in the outside world so that his/her familiar patterns work again. For example, Jimmy has a drinking and driving problem. As a result, Jimmy's parents prohibit Jimmy from using their car. As a response to this problem, Jimmy thinks, "My parents are annoying" and borrows a car from his friend and drinks and drives. Although this type of change may not be the type of change

Jimmy's parents were looking for, this occurs because Jimmy does not see the problem as his own problem. Rather, he sees the problem as something rooted in the outside world (i.e., his parents in this case). Of course, this type of change is usually not the type of change we are hoping for when we help someone develop.

If the person conceptualizes this as a problem in the outside world but cannot change anything in the outside world so that his/her familiar patterns work again, then the person may change his/her patterns temporarily with the hope that the situation will change and the old patterns will begin to work again. During this time the person feels like s/he is doing something s/he does not want to do and will lose energy as long as s/he sees the situation in this way. When the situation changes and the old patterns begin working again, the person simply reverts back to the old patterns. This type of change is usually not the type of change we are looking for either when we are helping someone change. For example, let us say that Jimmy's car privileges are temporarily revoked by his parents as a punishment for drinking and driving. Since Jimmy attributes the problem to his parents and not to himself, he may temporarily just drink and not drive, and wait until he can drink and drive with his parents' car again. Again, this type of change is usually not the type of change we are hoping for when we help someone develop.

On the other hand, if the person conceptualizes the problem as his/her own problem rather than a problem of the outside world, then the person becomes intrinsically motivated to change. In this case, even though the change was initialized by an outside force (something forcefully rattling us out of our patterns), the change is motivated from within. When this happens, not only does the person's patterns change but the person truly grows and develops. Even if the situation changes so that the old patterns work again, the person is not motivated to revert back to the old patterns because the person is a different person now (from the growth and development). Let us look at the example of Jimmy again. If Jimmy's car privileges are revoked and he attributes this problem to himself thinking, "it is my fault, I shouldn't drink and drive. I might kill others or kill myself. I won't drink and drive again", then he is more likely to actually change his patterns and stop drinking and driving with his parent's car even if he has the opportunity to drive it again. If this happens, Jimmy lets go of his desire to drink and drive and no longer separates his desires from his parent's desires (to stop driving drunk). He accepts the event (i.e., his parents telling him not to drink and drive and taking the car away from him) and allows the event to influence and change him.

Even though this may make sense from a theoretical standpoint, most of us would be surprised if Jimmy actually responded in this way. This is because we rarely attribute the problem to ourselves when others use the forceful method of helping us change because the very act of being forceful invites resistance and defensiveness. And the psychological state of being resistant and defensive, by definition, causes people to attribute problems onto other people and things rather than themselves. When we rattle people out of their comfort zones, we automatically make them defensive (i.e., their shells harden). This makes it very difficult for others to break through their shells and influence them in any way. In other words, the forceful way is a way to steal large amounts of energy. When we have large amounts of energy stolen, we naturally respond by becoming self-protective and hardening our shells and oftentimes stealing energy back from the environment. As mentioned earlier, this does not lead to true growth and maturation. But realistically, from our experiences, we know that the forceful way sometimes works. What actually happens when the forceful way works? This is the topic of the next section.

WHEN FORCING OTHERS TO GROW WORKS

The forceful way to change other people sometimes works. When it does work? What is the process? When we truly change people by being forceful, one of two things usually happens. One of these things is a reversal in perception. This happens when we force others to do things so much that they are forced to change their perceptions of their own behavior. From the perspective of the person being forced to change, interpreting the situation as being forced to do something that we do not want to do is quite disempowering. It makes us feel like we are being controlled by others and weak (i.e., it makes us lose energy). Thus, if we are forced to do something, we often subconsciously change our interpretation and start thinking, "I am doing this not because I am forced to do this. I am doing this because I want to do it". Basically, we change our desires so that it matches what has, is, or might happen. This change in perception empowers us and makes us feel like we are in control of our own behaviors. When this happens, we truly change. Because we think that we are doing this because we want to, we continue the behavior even when we are no longer forced to do it.

Let us look at an example. Terence's parents grounded him for staying out past his curfew. As a punishment, Terence is force to engage in volunteer church activities for three months. Because thinking that his parents have forced him to engage in volunteer church activity is disempowering for him, Terence changes his interpretation of the situation. Instead of thinking, "I hate this but I am being forced to do this," he thinks, "I am doing this because I want to do it. I am doing this because I believe it is a good thing to do. This makes me feel like I am a good person. This makes me feel accepted by others." By changing his interpretation of his behavior, he feels empowered. He feels like he is in charge and he is not being forced to do anything. Although sometimes we say these things to ourselves just to rationalize, when we truly feel this way, we truly really change. Because Terence thinks that he is doing this because he wants to, he continues the behavior even when he is no longer forced to do it.

Therefore, this change occurs when change our interpretation of the event. We are now doing something because we desire to do it rather than because we are forced to do it. If we use the ocean analogy, both ways described above involves pouring water onto the person you are trying to change to the point that they are almost completely filled with water and have almost no air inside of them (because water is poured in, their shells harden, and the person sinks). Because of the extreme discomfort we experience (no air/energy), we are forced to open up our pores so that we do not completely sink and drown in the water (i.e., allowing the other person or event to influence us). When we open our pores, our shells soften and we begin floating up and water naturally seeps out of our pores (i.e., more air inside). True development occurs when we open up our pores and expand our self-system.

A simpler example of this is when a person who is forced to change finds the new state intrinsically rewarding. For example, Shanna who hates carrots is forced to eat carrots. Upon being forced to eat the carrots she does not like, she realizes that she enjoys the taste of carrots. She thinks, "I feel good when I eat this vegetable. I don't have to avoid it anymore." In this case, the person was initially forced to do something but the real root of the change is in her own will. She no longer feels forced to eat carrots anymore. She likes eating carrots now. It is intrinsically rewarding for her to do so. She has opened up some of her pores and is less self-protective than before. Although this is a trivial example, this is true development. The next paragraphs examine more substantial changes of this sort.

If we initially find that the forceful way does not work, we can try one of two things. Use the patient method, which will be discussed in the next section, or use even more force (even after they resist). Regardless of how hard the shell has become, we can try to use even more force to break through the shell. This is what we do when we confront people denying their life threatening addiction to drugs. This is what Drill Sergeants do in bootcamps. This is commonly considered to be the last option when we face people who are either extremely dangerous to others or in extreme danger themselves[30].

Once the shell is broken, the person is forced to change. We push them to the point where they can no longer deny that the problem they are facing is their own. This is usually a very painful and devastating experience for the person and considerable effort is needed help them reconstruct their self-system again. Thus, from an ethical standpoint, if we are going to break their shells, we must also be ready and willing to help them rebuild a new and more adaptive one. Although it is not healthy to develop thick shells, everyone has a shell (we only vary in the thickness of the shell) that they live in (to support their self-system). In this sense, a shell is like a relatively closed system that includes many of our patterns that enable us to satisfy our desires. If we break someone's shell to help them grow out of their patterns, we must also be responsible enough to help them rebuild new patterns that enable them to satisfy their desires (i.e., experience energy) more effectively. This is the true meaning of tough love. This is the true meaning of acting responsibly in our relationships.

Thus, after we break people's shell, we must help them by being attentive and respectful to allow them to experience harmony with us. The point of breaking someone's shell is to enable them to experience harmony with more things than before and one of the things that we would like the person to experience more harmony with is our selves. In order to help them experience more harmony with ourselves, we must open up and be attentive and respectful toward them after we have broken their shell. Of course, it is impossible to be highly attentive and respectful when we break someone's shell (we would not be breaking the other person's shell if we were respectful and attentive). However, we must become attentive and respectful after we have broken someone's shell. If the person goes back to the previous shell after we think we have broken his/her shell and have become attentive and respectful toward him/her, then we know that we have not really broken his/her shell. If on the other hand, the person opens up and changes his/her patterns so that it incorporates the experience that broke their shell, then we could say that the person has really broken out of their shell. Even though it may seem quite systematic, using the forceful way to help someone change is truly an art. It is sometimes referred to as "tough love". We must know when to be tough and how tough we should be, and when to open up and be soft again. Figure 17 is a diagram illustrating this process of helping the other person grow in a forceful manner.

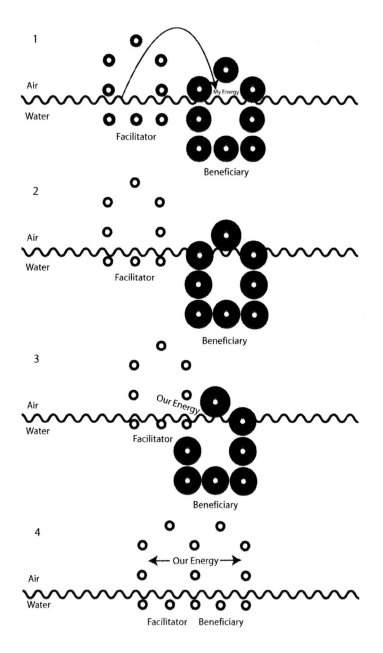

Figure 17. Helping Others Grow using Force

On the other hand, if we want someone to change but do not wish to experience harmony with him/her, we must not try to change him/her at all (and definitely not use the forceful method). If we are breaking someone's shell even though we do not wish to experience harmony with that person, we are merely being hurtful (and not attentive and respectful). We are merely stealing energy from the other person in this case. As mentioned earlier, this type of behavior is selfish, irresponsible and unhelpful even if we rationalize by thinking that we are doing this to help the other person.

HELPING PEOPLE GROW

The other school of thought concerning how to help other people develop is the patient way. This method focuses on providing an environment that is caring and safe so that the person is not afraid to face his/her defenses (i.e., soften their shells). The idea behind this approach is to send the other person a message saying, "I am here for you no matter what happens" and help them feel unafraid to allow the painful experience to influence them. The reason why we are afraid of this is that the mere act of allowing a painful experience to influence us does not feel pleasant (we lose energy). Therefore feeling unity and togetherness with others (and thereby perceiving that we have more energy) makes us become courageous to allow the painful experience to influence us (even though it is still unpleasant). It is like opening our pores and allowing the air to move in and out freely even if some of the air is lost by facing the painful experience. We don't feel as scared to lose the air from the painful experience because we feel that we have more air now (because of the unity we feel with the other person). We can be more courageous when someone is on our side. When we are anxious, our pores close up to protect all of the air (i.e., energy) we have. Because we are trying to protect the energy we have and facing our painful experience would make us lose energy (we lose energy when we do something we do not want to do), we avoid facing it. If, however, we are in a safe environment and we feel that someone is with us regardless of what happens (i.e., unity with the other person), we can open up our pores (at least the pores on one side to share the energy with that particular person). If we open up our pores, we can eventually experience more energy even if some of the energy (i.e., air) is temporarily lost by allowing the painful experience to influence us (i.e., allowing water to come inside). The opening of our pores caused by the supportive environment sometimes gives us the courage to allow things to influence us and let go of our defenses (see Figure 18).

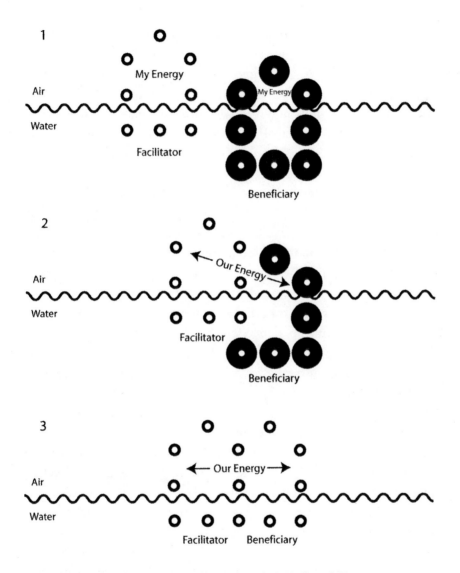

Figure 18. Helping Others Soften their Shells and Grow

Although we only learn and grow when we are ready (as mentioned in a previous section), providing this environment maximizes the person's opportunity to grow[31]. In many cases, a person's anxiety may be so strong that just providing a caring and supportive environment for a day or two may not be sufficient to soften his/her shell. Furthermore, there may be forces more powerful outside of the relationship between you and the person you are trying to help that prevents him/her from feeling safe. As many people say, patience and hope may be the most valuable of virtues. This may be especially true when we want to be helpful in the development of any individual (including ourselves). In most cases, if we remain respectful and caring for long enough, the person will eventually be ready for the next step.

One thing is for sure. No one wants to live the rest of his/her lives in anxiety. Some may have given up because they see no hope. But if we have the opportunity, we would always choose peace and freedom over anxiety. We all have a natural motivation to become free of anxieties. If we are given the right type of environment, we often take that opportunity to face the painful experiences that are causing our anxieties and stop protecting ourselves from them. Once we let go of our desires and we accept the painful experience (see Figure 11), it no longer bothers us. Once this happens, we integrate the painful experience into our own understanding of our selves and the world around us. When we do this, we rebuild new patterns that enable us to satisfy our own desires (i.e., experience energy) more effectively. When we get to this stage, we intuitively understand the former patterns we used to use and can relate to the people who use patterns similar to that. However, we now have different and more effective patterns. This is the development of wisdom. This is why individuals who have overcome many hardships in life are very understanding of others. They understand others because they have been there before. They know the patterns of other people very well and they also know how (or at least one way) to break out of these patterns because they have done so themselves. Individuals like this tend to take the role of role models and mentors in society (though not always as official occupations).

This is why painful experiences can affect our development in both positive and negative ways. As mentioned in earlier sections, painful experiences can affect our development negatively. Painful experiences deplete us of energy. Painful experiences make us harden our shells to protect us from the pain/anxiety. Painful experiences make us develop patterns of protecting and stealing energy. However, once we overcome these painful experiences by letting go of our desires associated with the painful experience, the same experiences can make us understanding, empathic, wise and experienced. If a person allows the painful experience to truly influence him/her, the person naturally adapts to that and uses this experience to learn from (and creates patterns in his or her self-system more effective than before). When this happens, the painful experience makes the person understanding, empathic, and wise. If, on the other hand, the person resists and shuts the painful experience out by placing them inside their shell, the person sinks in the ocean and becomes depleted of energy and develops patterns of protecting and stealing energy.

Helping others grow is a noble but difficult endeavor. We need to know how much to take, when to take, and we also need to know how much to give, and when to give. Sometimes we need to be gentle in order to help others grow and sometimes we need to be honest. Although people commonly say that honesty is important in relationships, what does this really mean? Let's examine the meaning of honesty in this context.

HONESTY AND SINCERITY

Although many people say that honesty is important in relationships, it is an expression commonly misunderstood. The term, "honesty" in this expression refers to being our true self (and therefore being true to others) and not merely being open to others about our expressions of anxiety. We sometimes rationalize our behaviors of stealing energy by convincing ourselves that we are being honest and that being honest is a good thing. We all know that we can be very hurtful and aggressive and interpret this as being honest. However, this is not what people mean when they say that we should be honest in our relationships.

Perhaps a better word for this would be "sincerity". It may be more appropriate to say that sincerity is important in relationships. An easy way to distinguish mere honesty from sincerity is to think of the motivation behind our behaviors. If the motivation behind the behavior is to protect our own energy or to steal energy from the other person, it is not sincerity even though it may be interpreted as honesty. If on the other hand, the motivation behind the behavior is to develop or maintain a sense of unity with the other person, it is sincerity. What is important is to care about the other person even when we are the main person receiving energy. This is the essence of sincerity. This is the essence of unity. This is the essence of a smooth relationship. This is what makes us truly wise.

In some cases, people may not say what is on their mind (even though they may believe that it is the truth) out of respect for the other person's feelings. In some cases, we may even be forced to say something that we don't believe in ourselves out of respect for the other person's feelings. This is part of being sincere even though it may not be considered honest. When we know that the truth is hurtful to others we try to break it to them gently if we truly care about them. We wait for the right moment to tell them. We think of the right words to use and the right emotional expressions to use. This is sincerity. This is what is important in relationships. Sometimes, this may be interpreted as honesty and sometimes this may be interpreted as dishonesty, but it will always be interpreted as loving and caring if it is done with sincerity.

Sometimes, it is difficult to tell whether we are being sincere or honest. One way to determine whether we are being sincere or not is by examining whether we are willing to change ourselves for that other person. If we are not willing to change for that person, and want to change that person into what we want them to be like, we are not being sincere (even though we may be behaving honestly). However, if we are open and accepting of the other person and willing to change ourselves for that other person, we are most likely being sincere.

In order to develop the conscious ability to tell when it is appropriate to be honest and when it is not and in order to consciously understand what it means to be sincere, we need to have a well-developed understanding of not only how relationships work but an understanding of ourselves and how we relate to the world. We need to have a philosophy of life that makes sense of how we are embedded in the multiple relationships we are involved in. Although we have covered some of the theoretical aspects of this work already, let's focus a little more on the bigger picture, the philosophical implications of all of this.

Philosophical Implications

AWARENESS, FREEDOM, AND RESPONSIBILITY

When we become aware of our interpersonal patterns or the dynamics of our relationships or how the bigger picture looks, we begin having the freedom to choose. For example, if I become aware of my tendency to use the aloofness/charisma behavior pattern on my friends, I can choose not to do it the next time I am tempted to use this behavior pattern. Before I became aware of this, however, I did not have this choice. Before I became aware of this, I automatically reacted to situations and used aloofness/charisma to steal energy from others. If you are not aware of what you are doing and are acting according to your subconscious tendencies, you have no freedom. You just do what you have been conditioned to do from your past experiences without being aware of it. Thus, the more awareness you develop (about yourself, others and the environment), the more awareness you have of your choices. The more awareness you have of your choices, the more freedom you have. We must remember, however, that with freedom comes responsibility.

Once we realize that we have a choice, we are responsible for the choices we make. If I see that I have a choice of stepping on your toes or not stepping on your toes and I choose to step on your toes, you would consider me as responsible for stepping on your toes. If, however, I accidentally step on your toes because I lost my balance, you may not consider me as responsible for stepping on your toes. If we perceive that a person has choice and chooses to do something over something else, we hold them responsible for their actions. This works the same way with our own actions. If we consciously choose to do something, we see ourselves as responsible for the choice we make. If we just react with our subconscious tendencies according to what we have been conditioned to do, we do not see ourselves as responsible for our own actions. This is why we sometimes say, "He does these annoying things but he is a good person and he means well". We have the tendency to forgive people who steal energy without conscious awareness but do not forgive those who steal energy intentionally.

One of the most important aspects of human development is the development of awareness. This includes awareness of how the world works and how you relate to it. It is, in a sense, the development of the self-system. And as discussed earlier, the development of awareness implies development of freedom and choice. And the more freedom and choice we have, the more responsibility we have for making the choices that we make. Thus, the more we develop, the more awareness we have, the more freedom we have, and the more responsibility we have.

If we take this one step further, we discover that development of awareness is a wonderful thing. If we are miserable, we can develop awareness of why we are miserable and make a choice about what to do to make us happier. If there is something that we do not like about our lives, we can learn and develop our awareness to understand why we do not like it and choose to change things so that we will be happier. We may not be able to change things immediately but we can at least begin working on it if you are aware of what is wrong and what it is that you want to change.

The scary thing is that, once we develop that awareness and freedom, it is our responsibility to do something about it. It allows us no excuse to stay miserable, complain, and blame others. Sometimes we are so comfortable having other people and things to blame for our misery that we do not want to change. This sometimes, prevents us from growing and developing awareness. This is how we get stuck into patterns of stealing energy. We become comfortable with our patterns even though we are not truly happy. As the psychologist Erich Fromm has written in his book "Escape from Freedom", being in charge of our lives is a heavy responsibility[32]. It leaves us with no one to blame but ourselves for the quality of our lives. We often are terrified to take the responsibility of being in charge of our lives because of this. This is what happens when we stop growing and developing as human beings. We are essentially refusing to take responsibility for our lives and there-fore, we stop growing.

If we take this even one step further, it means that blaming anything other than our selves for what happens with our lives is the same thing as refusing to grow. It is often used as an excuse not to grow and develop. We all have the tendency to think, "This person or situation is preventing me from doing what I want (which is what you assume will make you grow and mature and be a happy person)." In the same way, even if we are aware of our choices and we refuse to make a choice, we are just trying to escape the responsibility that comes with that choice. As painful as this may sound (because we all do this to some extent), blaming anything other than our selves is always an excuse for not growing up and taking responsibility.

Awareness is important because it provides us with the potential to break free from our patterns because it allows us to see things from a wider and deeper perspective. This implies that any one experience can be inter-preted in multiple ways. The mind can build many pitfalls in our lives but at the same time, the mind can be a wonderful tool. This is why the same event can make one person miserable while making the other person feel absolutely great! Let's examine this wonderful tool and how it works.

MATTER OF MIND: IT'S ALL RELATIVE

As we have seen from the previous section, most emotions that we experience in life depend on how we perceive things (i.e., the bound-aries and associations we make). Just as we can see a glass as half full or half empty, we interpret any sensory information in various different ways. We commonly say that the person who sees the glass as half empty feels more negative than the person who sees the glass as half full. This means that depending on how we perceive our experiences in our lives, we can feel very differently. One the other hand if we feel negative, we tend to perceive things in a negative way. If we feel positive on the other hand, we tend to perceive things in a positive way. The point here is that emotion and perception occur together. They are two aspects of the same thing. If you feel positive, you will have the tendency to perceive things in a positive way. If you feel a negative, you will have the tendency to perceive things in a negative way. Conversely, if you think positively, you will have the tendency to feel positively. And if you think negatively, you will have the tendency to feel negatively.

This is because there are holons in the mind as well as in physical space. The giving and taking of energy in the physical world is very easy to understand. We can objectively sense the energy being released when some holon is broken down. A rock may hit another rock and break it. The broken rock released energy in the process of breaking down (just like atoms broken down to release nuclear energy). The giving and taking of energy in the biological world is also fairly easy to understand. Organisms eat other organisms to take the energy from one another and make them their own (just like we eat apples and fish).

Holons in the mind, however, are much more complicated. With holons in the mind, we give and take energy symbolically. Even though it seems like you are not really giving or taking energy because it is not anything we can objectively sense, we can experientially sense a loss or a gain in energy. This is what I refer to as the exchange of energy throughout most of this book. This psychological energy is like all other physical energy. It works just like physical energy. It is just energy of the mind. It comes and goes from our symbolic interpretations and associations that we make in our minds. Energy influences our biological state, oftentimes relating to our health. We all know that stress, which is our conventional term for loss of energy, influences our physical health in very important ways. Although we have the tendency to feel that the stuff in our mind is not real and only a symbolic representation of the real world, the mind is something very real and it influences our physical state in very important ways.

Although it is possible to directly change our emotional experience in order to think differently, it is often easier to change our thoughts in order to change how we feel. Many psychologists discuss how we can change our thought patterns in order to change our emotional experiences[33]. We have discussed the idea of examining the importance of our desires and letting go of our desires in previous sections and we know that it influences our emotional experiences.

The notion of changing the way we think to make us feel differently also applies to our experiences of giving and taking energy. The same event can be interpreted as giving or taking energy depending on how we interpret the information. Let's examine this by recalling the example of Dana and Holly discussed earlier. Dana and Holly are in a dating relationship. Holly is just getting over a difficult relationship with an abusive spouse who used to bring her red roses all of the time. Dana does not know this and takes the liberty to bring Holly some red roses on their date as a kind and caring gesture (thinking that Holly desires roses). Seeing the red roses, Holly is reminded of her former abusive relationship and assumes that Dana heard about her former relationship and was doing this to make her feel uncomfortable. Holly becomes extremely upset at this and begins yelling at Dana. In this case, Dana perceives the event of Dana bringing Holly some red roses as Dana giving energy to Holly. Holly on the other hand, perceives the same event as Dana taking energy from Holly. One perceives the event as giving and the other perceives the same event as taking. If Dana had taken Holly's perspective by finding out about her former relationship, he would not have brought her the roses and nobody would have been upset. If Holly takes Dana's perspective, there is no need for her to become anxious. Thus, changing perspectives can change our emotional experiences as well as the behaviors that lead to the emotional experiences a great deal.

Another important factor concerning how our perceptions influence our emotions is where we draw our boundaries in our experiences and which side of the boundary we identify with. For example, if I buy a lottery ticket I end up losing even though some stranger wins, I may not be extremely happy. However, if that person who won the lottery was my son, I may be extremely happy. In both cases, it is someone else who one the lottery but my emotional experience is very different. This is because, in my mind, I draw a boundary between my self and the stranger (who won the lottery) even though I do not draw as much of a boundary between my self and my son (who won the lottery). I perceive my son and I to be together or united in many ways and therefore whatever happens to my son feels like something that is happening to me (to a certain extent). In contrast, I do not feel the same type of togetherness or unity with the stranger who won the lottery. Therefore what happens to the stranger does not feel like something that is happening to me. If I find out later that this stranger who won the lottery is my long lost son, I may become extremely happy even though I wasn't before. This is because I have dissolved the boundary between my self and the stranger (to a certain extent). Now I feel as though whatever happens to the stranger (long lost son) is something that happens to me to a certain extent. In this case I have rearranged the boundaries so that the stranger is no longer a stranger.

This is the same reason why you feel hurt when someone in your family is insulted. Since you have a relatively thin boundary between you and your family member, whatever happens to the other person feels like something that is happening to you. In contrast, the person who insulted your family member may be seen as someone outside of that boundary that includes you and your family member. This makes one feel like the insulter has taken energy from the entity that includes you and your family member and therefore you feel hurt. If you draw a boundary between you and your family member and thus feel no sense of togetherness or unity with your family member, the insult to your family member may not bother you.

The question of where we draw our boundaries also has an important implication on what we compare events/objects /persons to. If I draw the boundary between what happened and something more positive that might have happened, I feel upset. If I draw the boundary between what happened and something more negative that might have happened, I feel very fortunate and happy. If a family member is injured in a car accident, we can feel glad that the person did not die from the accident or we can feel upset that the person is not as healthy as he or she used to be. If my teenage daughter does not come home before 3:00am, I may be upset that she stayed out so late or I may be glad that she came home safely. This works the same way with people and objects. If I compare my son's running speed with Olympic runners, I may be unhappy with my son's running ability. If I compare my house with a luxury mansion, I may be unhappy with it. Most of us, however, do not make extreme types of comparisons like these and therefore are able to regulate our emotions reasonably well.

As we have seen, where we draw our boundaries, often influences how we feel. People who can draw boundaries in certain spots are people who feel happy in their lives. People who can draw boundaries in certain spots have the wonderful ability to remain grateful of the many experiences life has to offer. These people also tend to have the great ability to forgive people, regardless of what happens. Let us look at these characteristics in further detail.

GRATEFULNESS AND FORGIVENESS

People who are grateful of all of their experiences in life are happy people. They draw boundaries in the right places. When we are grateful, we compare our experiences (i.e., what happens) with the negative things that might or have occurred. I may appreciate that I have a roof over my head because I compare it to not having a roof over my head.

I may be happy that my daughter came home safely because I compare it to my daughter coming home hurt in some way. I am grateful for my health because I compare it with being ill. I appreciate having a computer that works well because I compare it with having a broken computer. This is why developing a great appreciation (a sense of gratefulness) for all of our experiences is in many ways a key to happiness. People who are grateful are happy and being happy makes us grateful. Furthermore, being happy makes us forgiving and the act of forgiving makes us happy. It is all a positive cycle.

Intuitively, we all know that forgiving people not only sets other people (i.e., the people we are upset with) free but also makes ourselves happier. The act of forgiving rids ourselves of conflict and makes us feel at peace with ourselves. When we are upset at others and have difficulty forgiving them, it is because we have separated what they did and what we wanted them to do (i.e., our desires). Forgiving is the act of letting go of what we wanted them to do or not do (i.e., our desires). When we let go of our desires (i.e., what we wanted them to do), we can naturally accept what the other person did. In contrast, as long as we hold on to our desires (i.e., what we wanted them to do), we can never get rid of the separation between what really happened and what we wanted to have happen (i.e., our desires). And if we cannot get rid of that separation, our mind stays in conflict and conflict in these particular situations is the same as not being able to forgive. Since we cannot change the past, we cannot change what happened. And because we cannot change what happened, the only way to get rid of this separation is to let go of our desire (i.e., accept what the other person did). Some theorists may argue that we can also change our desires so that they match what happened (i.e., interpret the other person's past behavior as something we actually desired). However, in order to change our desires so that they match with what happened, one needs to let go of our initial desires in the first place. Thus in any case, we need to let go of our desires that conflict with what really happened.

Let's look at an example. A woman may have difficulty forgiving her husband for having an affair. As long as she holds on to her desire to have a faithful husband who does not cheat on her, she cannot forgive her. As soon as she lets go of that desire, she can accept what happened because there is nothing in her mind that is in conflict with it. Alternatively, she may relieve herself of her conflict by changing her desires. If she thinks that this was an event that was meant to occur so that she learns a valuable lesson to further her development, she is no longer in conflict with what happened. She no longer resists what really happened. In this case, she has changed her perceptions and now desires what really happened (i.e., her husband having an affair) because this enabled her to learn a valuable lesson that enabled her to develop more as a person. In both cases, however, she had to let go of her initial desire to have a faithful husband who does not cheat on her and this has lead her to forgive.

As we have seen, how we experience boundaries influences how we feel to a large extent. However, sometimes experiencing boundaries has no (or very little) emotional effect on us while at other times, experiencing boundaries affects our emotions deeply. Why do some boundaries affect our emotions more than other boundaries? The next section is an examination of this issue.

"MERE CONFLICT", "MY CONFLICT", AND "OUR CONFLICT"

Regardless of whether the conflict is perceived within you or with something in the outside world, differentiation and boundaries are always necessary for conflict to occur. Conflict can only be experienced when we separate ourselves from something else and perceive things as separate entities. Sometimes, we perceive conflict that does not involve ourselves. As long as I do not identify with either of the entities, the conflict is not stressful (i.e., anxiety producing) because it is not *my conflict.* It is just *mere conflict* and not *my conflict.* The moment we identify with one side, we begin experiencing anxiety or excitement from the conflict. Let us look at an example. Suppose I watch two football teams playing a game with each other. I am not very familiar with these two football teams and I do not particularly identify with either of them. In this case, I perceive conflict but I do not feel conflicted (i.e., I do not feel anxious or excited about it). It is *mere conflict.* If however, I begin identifying with one of the teams (team A) for some reason, I become self-conscious and the conflict becomes *my conflict.* I now want team A to win over team B. If team A is losing, I feel upset. If team A is winning, I may feel excited or I may feel anxious that team B might make a comeback. Either way, I am in conflict. The diagrams in Figure 19 are simple illustrations of the difference between *mere conflict* and *my (or our) conflict.*

Mere Conflict

My / Our Conflict

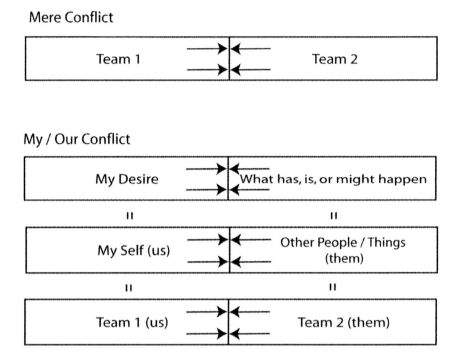

Figure 19. Mere Conflict vs. My/Our Conflict

In this case, we could say that it is not only *my conflict* but *our conflict* since I now identify with the whole team. If the team wins, I feel like I won. In fact, everyone in the teams feels like they have won. If the team loses, I feel like I have lost. What this means is that the conflict we have can be experienced not only individually but collectively as a group as well. It may be our desires vs. what happened, is happening, or might happen instead of my desire vs. what happened, is happening, or might happen. Now I may stop identifying with the team if it loses because it feels unpleasant afterwards. When this happens, I do not feel like I lost and therefore I do not have to feel any anxiety. I think, "They lost." instead of, "We lost." This implies that I can change the boundaries in order to regulate my emotions (e.g., if they lose, it is not *my* team anymore).

In some cases, this conflict is considered to be excitement (such as when we anticipate winning in a football game). In other cases, this conflict is considered to be anxiety (such as when we anticipate losing in a football game). As mentioned earlier, the experience of anxiety and excitement are two sides of the same coin. One does not exist without the other. We do not feel excited about realizing our desires if we there was no possibility of failing to realize our desires. In fact, they wouldn't be perceived as desires if there was no possibility of failing to realize them. In the same way, we do not feel anxious if there was no possibility of realizing our desires. In fact, we would not even have those desires if there was absolutely no possibility of realizing them. An important point here is that for every thought, there is a counterpart. The next section will examine this in further detail.

THE DUALITY OF THOUGHT AND EMOTION

We learned earlier that the concept of dogs exists because we experience things that are not dogs. In other words, learning what dogs are, is the same thing as learning to tell the difference betweens things that are dogs and things that are not dogs. You have learned to draw a boundary between different kinds of experiences. The same thing happens when you learn any other concept. The concept of peacefulness only exists because there are times when we are not peaceful. The concept of excitement exists because there are times we are excited and there are times we are not excited. If we all felt excited all of the time, the concept of excitement would not exist because there is nothing to distinguish it from. This happens because this is just the way our mind works from a cognitive perspective.

Emotions work in a similar way. Just as there are two ways to feel energized, there are two types of positive emotions. One set of positive emotions are characterized as excitement. These correspond to the experiences that make your heart beat faster in a positive way. From an experiential perspective, these emotions do not exist without their counterpart, which are the emotions associated with anxiety (i.e., negative excitement). In other words, these positive emotions only exist because there are negative emotions, not only because they need each other to distinguish themselves but because the actual experience of these emotions requires the experience of the other set of emotions (its counterparts). Let me explain this more. If we did not experience anxiety, we would not experience excitement since excitement is only experienced when anxiety is alleviated or when we anticipate the alleviation of anxiety.

Let's think of the times we were excited. We are never excited in situations where there is nothing to be anxious about (or worry about). When there is nothing to be anxious about (or worry about), we stay calm. There is no need to be excited. We are not motivated to change anything. Everything is just fine and there is no need to be worried or excited. We are only excited when there is or was some potential for something negative happening. And when there is some potential for something negative to occur, we experience anxiety in varying degrees as well. For example, we may feel excited that we won a soccer game. We are excited to win because there was the possibility of losing (i.e., a negative event). We may feel excited that we might win a soccer game in the future but this excitement only exists because there is a possibility of losing as well. In the same way, we may feel excited to succeed on a new project at work because there is also the possibility of failing. If there was no possibility of failing, and success was the only possible outcome, there is no anxiety (nothing to fear or worry about) and thus we would not be excited to succeed. In fact, we wouldn't even call this success. Therefore as the psychologists Stanley Schachter and Jerome Singer have suggested, positive and negative arousal (i.e., excitement and anxiety) are really the same in many ways[34]. They are two sides of the same coin. One cannot be experienced without the other. Just as dominance and submissiveness are two sides of the same coin (you only feel dominant when someone or something is being submissive and you only feel submissive when someone or something is dominating you), so are anxiety and excitement. Both of these sets of concepts correspond to the middle of the horizontal axis in Figure 3. Dominance and excitement correspond to the top and submissiveness and fear correspond to the bottom. Our mind perceives things so that we are in a constant rhythm of experiencing one after the other.

The other set of positive emotions is commonly characterized as peacefulness. These correspond to the experiences that sooth you and make you feel calm and relaxed. Although from a cognitive perspective, these emotions need other emotions to distinguish themselves from (such as anxiety and excitement), they do not have an experiential counterpart. The reason why they have no experiential counterpart is that the concept of complete peacefulness represents a perfect state of balance and harmony. Even though excitement and anxiety need each other to reach a state of balance, peacefulness requires nothing to reach a state of balance because it is already in a perfect state of balance. This is because the experience of excitement and anxiety is a product of one mode of operation that requires one to focus on boundaries whereas peacefulness is a product of another mode of operation that requires one to dissolve boundaries. The next section discusses these two modes of operation.

DIGITAL AND ANALOG MODES OF OPERATION

Whenever we experience things, we use a combination of two modes of operation. One is commonly labeled the digital mode and the other is commonly labeled as the analog mode. The digital mode of operation can be characterized as thought that focuses on categorization. When we think about things, we differentiate things in our experience such as objects, ideas, concepts, plans and procedures, people and behaviors. This book is different from this book. One is different from two. You are different from me. My desires or expectations are different from yours. My desire is different from what is happening. How I do this is different from how you do this. We don't often think about this but we often separate our own thoughts and body parts from ourselves as well. When I think, "I am tempted eat the cake but I know I shouldn't", I am separating what I want to do from what I might do. When I think, "my knee is bothering me", I am separating myself from the pain in my knee even though my knee (and its pain) is physically a part of me.

With this mode of functioning, we categorize things as separate. Many times we also go one step further and associate our desires with one side. I desire this book more than this other book. I desire this method more than this method. I desire eating this cake more than going on a diet. I desire for the pain in my knee to go away more than the pain in my knee to stay. If someone else desires the other method or another book or the pain staying in our knee or anything else that is separate from my desires, we immediately feel that the other person is on the other side. When this happens it becomes me vs. the other person. This is what happens when we compete for energy. This is what happens when someone else takes the other side (whether it is another team, another opinion, or our pain in the knee). They immediately become the opposition. This is the common, "I thought you were on my side" phenomenon.

Furthermore, we go one step further and try to make the one associated with our desires win over the other side. If we win, it makes me feel like my side is more powerful. The concept of winning and being powerful is analogous to taking energy from the other side. My desire for the pain in my knee to go away must win over the pain in my knee staying so that I can perform well in this basketball game. My team must win over your team. My desires must win over what has, is, or might happen. Once we identify our desires with one side, there is no tie game. Once we identify with one side in this mode of functioning, the only possible outcome is that one side wins and the other side loses. Needless to say, if those are the only possible outcomes, we want to be on the winning side. When the side we identify with is losing (i.e., losing energy to the other side), we feel fearful, anxious, and sometimes even worthless and depressed. We may feel this way when we feel we are losing our battle to fight our addiction to smoking (my desire to stop vs. my addiction). We may also feel this way when we lose our jobs (my desire to keep the job vs. my boss' desire to fire me). As we can see, this mode of functioning not only makes us categorize things, but makes us view things as a competition in many cases.

In sum, part of our mind is made to automatically separate and categorize things. In addition, we have the tendency to associate our desires with one side. The other side is commonly viewed as the opposition and we have a tendency to try to win against it (i.e., take energy from it). In the digital mode of thought, there is only black and white. There are no shades of gray. Things are organized in separate categories. Things are either in one category or another and we commonly identify with one of the categories (the one we associate our desires with). Furthermore, the category that we identify with must win (i.e., be powerful to take energy from the other categories). This is the digital mode of thought.

The digital mode of functioning is the earthly side of our selves. It motivates us to compete and survive. This mode of functioning is also what makes us planful, logical and analytical since planning, logic, and analysis require separation and differentiation. It enables us to differentiate what we desire and what has, is, or might happen. It is also the practical side of us that motivates us and helps us to physically survive. For example, it is useful to differentiate things we can eat from things we cannot eat. It is also useful to differentiate a cat from a lion. These differentiations are based on the differentiations between our desires and what might happen (e.g., I desire to live vs. I might die if I eat this or I might be hurt if I approach this lion). This mode of functioning not only helps us survive, but is the source of our motivation to survive (because it makes us think life is better than death). The digital mode of functioning corresponds to the middle of horizontal dimension in Figure 3. When this mode of functioning dominates our thinking, we are in a state of separation and differentiation. This mode of functioning is also the basis of competition (i.e., giving vs. taking). Although biologically, various parts of the brain correspond to these functions, we notice that this roughly corresponds to the functions of the left cerebral hemisphere of the brain (for most right handed people).

The analog mode of operation can be characterized as thought that focuses on putting things together to form larger wholes. It enables us to understand relationships between things, both spacially and temporally. This is the mode we primarily use when we engage in artistic and intuitive types of behavior such as music, art, poetry, and dance. The silent moment between two drumbeats has little meaning if it is not in the context of all of the other drumbeats. A spot of white has little meaning without the context of all of the other colors in the painting. The analog mode brings the world together and allows us to experience things in unity and togetherness. It enables us to see how things relate to each other to form larger wholes. And if things go together well, this mode of functioning allows us to experience unity, harmony, and beauty. Things are experienced as going together well when we experience harmony and balance in some way. We experience beauty when two musical notes are in harmony (i.e., when sound waves are in harmony). We experience beauty when two colors in a painting or scenery are in harmony (i.e., when light waves are in harmony). The more harmony and balance we experience, the more heavenly and spiritual it feels.

This is one reason why the analog mode of functioning is often associated with the realm of the divine. It is the mode of functioning that enables us to be spontaneous and intuitive (such as when we are singing in the shower without a care in the world or deeply meditating in our bedroom). It is the mode of functioning that enables us to experience times when everything is clicking (or in continuous flow). It is the part of us that enables us to experience unity and harmony. Many people describe this experience as mysterious, graceful, spiritual, mystical, or out of this world. When this mode of functioning dominates, we approach a state of unity and everything seems to flow smoothly (we do not divide time into separate moments). We are paying attention to almost everything around us and almost everything around us is attending to us simultaneously at every single moment. It seems that energy in the universe is always in a continuous flow and the more we are in touch with this mode of functioning, the more synchronized we are with the general energy flow of the universe. This is often manifested as spontaneous, graceful, caring, and loving behavior. Some have described this type of experience as just "being" or "the true self". The analog mode of functioning corresponds to the right end of horizontal dimension in Figure 3 where we simultaneously give and take equal amounts of energy from each other (this is the experience of being in sync with everything around us). Although we may not be able to experience complete unity consciousness, this may be the closest possible experience to it that we may reach in our lifetime.

Although biologically, various parts of the brain correspond to these functions, we notice that this roughly corresponds to the functions of the left cerebral hemisphere (for most right handed people: Left handed people vary in the lateralization and specialization of the cerebral hemispheres). These two modes of functioning correspond to many of the central dichotomies we experience in life such as love/play vs. work/business or emotion/intuition vs. logic/analysis, the heart vs. the head, integration vs. differentiation, subjective/relational vs. objective/detached, and art vs. science. In all of these dichotomies, the former corresponds to the analog mode of functioning and the latter correspond to the digital mode of functioning. Furthermore, although they seem slightly different, dichotomies such as stability vs. change and order vs. chaos also correspond to these two modes of functioning. Stability and order is a state of unity where things are in harmony and things seem to be in a continuous flow. On the other hand, when things are seen as separate, choppy and in conflict with each other, we experience change. And if this experience is extreme, we describe it as chaos (e.g., giving and taking extreme amounts of energy). Furthermore, only when we differentiate two states (which corresponds to the digital mode) can we experience change (thus one state is perceived to change into another). In sum, the analog mode enables us to integrate with the environment and allows us to experience the bigger picture first hand. It also allows us to understand the specific things and parts (such as our individual selves) in relation to the larger whole. On the other hand, the digital mode enables us to preserve our own integrity and allows us to understand the components that make up the larger whole (big picture) by dividing it into smaller parts.

It is important to note that we are never completely in one mode of functioning. Although we may use one mode of functioning more than the other at a given moment, we are always using a combination of the two. From a biological perspective, although there are times when one hemisphere is more active than the other, both hemispheres are always used in combination with each other. We are never in complete unity and we are never in a state of complete separation. Furthermore, there may be individual differences concerning which mode we use more in general. Although it may not be as simple as it is typically portrayed, the people who use the analog mode more often (commonly called right brained) may seem spontaneous and intuitive and the people who use the digital mode more often (commonly called left brained) may seem to be more logical and analytical.

As mentioned earlier, the digital mode of functioning roughly corresponds to chaos and the analog mode of functioning roughly corresponds to stability. In life we have a rhythm of stability and chaos as we experience a repetition of facing new challenges and then feeling comfortable after adapting to the challenge and then facing other new challenges and adapting to those new challenges again. This is part of the rhythm of nature. The rhythm of nature, however, can be appreciated in various other ways as well.

THE RHYTHM OF NATURE

As we have seen from the previous sections, rhythm is evident in all aspects of nature. We not only experience rhythm in our relationships but everywhere in nature. In many places around the world, we have the four seasons repeating themselves over and over every year. Within that larger rhythm, we experience a monthly rhythm with the moon and the tides (women also experience this with their hormonal cycle). Within that monthly rhythm, we repeat smaller rhythms such as the rhythm of day and night. Within the rhythm of day and night, we have smaller rhythms of inhaling and exhaling. And this can go on and on. There is rhythm within rhythm within rhythm. Nature is rhythm and rhythm is nature. Life is rhythm. Existence is rhythm.

Everything seems to have a rhythm of giving and receiving as we have discussed earlier. At first, there also seems to be a larger rhythm that makes the rhythm of giving and receiving smoother and then rougher, and then smoother and then rougher just like the tides becoming bigger and then smaller and then bigger and then smaller again. But then we notice that this second type of rhythm is the same rhythm seen from a different perspective. When the rhythm of giving and receiving in a relationship is rough, we pay more attention to it (i.e., we give more energy) just as we pay more attention to two people fighting rather than two people in harmony. Conversely, when it is smooth, we do not attend to it even though it is attending to us (i.e., we receive more energy). Therefore, it is easier to attract attention from a couple in peace with each other than a couple in a fight. Basically, we are in a rhythm of giving and receiving energy with a relationship. In other words, we are involved *in* a relationship *with* a relationship. Thus, if we really think about it, this second type of rhythm boils down to a rhythm of giving and receiving as well[35].

It seems that we feel more comfortable when our rhythm matches the rhythm of the environment. In other words, adjusting our rhythm to the rhythm of the environment enables us to feel more comfortable in the various situations we encounter in our lives. Because we cannot completely stop the rhythm and achieve perfect harmony as living beings, the best thing to do may be to adjust our rhythm so that our rhythm is in sync with the rhythm of the rest of nature (including other people). The more we do this, the more we feel whole, peaceful, and full of energy. It is like clapping in same rhythm with everyone else in the crowd. When our rhythm is not in sync with the rest of nature, we feel alienated, anxious, fearful but sometimes positively excited as well (because we feel like rebels). It is like not being able to clap with the same timing as everyone else in the crowd. This can make us feel alienated and anxious but it can also make us feel excited and rebellious. This may be one of the reasons why people love listening to and dancing to music. It makes it easy for us to feel in sync with the rhythm of the environment.

GIRLS AND BOYS

Perhaps we can make some rough associations between the theoretical framework discussed here and archetypical images relating to masculinity and femininity. Archetypical images of things fluid, circular, balanced, continuous and connected are commonly associated with femininity. In many cultures, women are associated with earth, life, and rhythm. Thus we have the terms "Mother Earth" and "Mother Nature". Men, in contrast, are associated with the absence of rhythm. Archetypical images of things static, linear, separate are commonly considered to be masculine in nature. Concepts associated with the absence of rhythm such as complete dominance, destruction, and death (no rhythm, or destruction of rhythm) are commonly associated with men.

The general archetypical image of women represents nature, life, and rhythm. Women give birth, women experience menstrual cycles, women enjoy the rhythmic process of conversation. Women in general seem to be more familiar with the rhythm of life. Thus, women seem to be more comfortable being part of the rhythm of nature. Nature seems to be their home. Because nature is their home, they feel more comfortable with rhythmic experiences, human interaction, conversation, music (dance), the menstrual cycle, visual patterns (which in many ways is analogous to rhythm) and beauty in general (often defined by rhythm and balance).

Thus the archetypical image on women may relate to the middle ground between the center and right end of the diagram in Figure 3. This area represents the experience of neither being completely separate nor being completely united, but experiencing a natural rhythm of giving and taking of energy. It is a state of being somewhat analog but also somewhat digital. And because nature has this natural rhythm similar to this, women feel at home with nature. This may be one reason why matriarchical societies generally tend to be more peaceful and egalitarian than patriarchical societies.

The archetypical image of men is linear, static, and separate. They are all related to the digital mode of functioning. Men seem to have more difficulty adjusting to the rhythm of life. They do not seem to have the type of familiarity with rhythm that women seem so comfortable with. Men seem to be more familiar with states with no rhythm. Perhaps their home is the state of complete unity as in the state we are in before birth. Because life and physical existence consists of rhythm, it is as though men feel like they are in an unfamiliar place throughout life. This makes them feel alienated and anxious. These feelings motivate them to cause some change (to escape this state). This can never be completely achieved in life because, by definition, life is rhythm. Death is an escape from this and perhaps this is why boys have higher infant mortality rates than girls and men have shorter life expectancy rates than women. This may also be why men have higher suicide rates than women.

Alternatively, many men try to return to the state of no rhythm and complete stability by completely dominating and destroying rhythm even though rhythm is never destroyed. Many acts of extreme violence that are in the majority committed by men may be considered attempts to destroy rhythm. Men may conquer, kill, or threaten to destroy rhythm. Men destroy nature. Men wage wars. Men try to dominate and win over things in order to destroy rhythm. Unfortunately, these attempts are never successful in destroying rhythm, because existence, by definition, implies rhythm. When we dominate something, it dominates us back. This is the rhythm of nature. We can never completely dominate anything forever. Nature occurs in rhythms. The more we dominate something, the more it dominates us back.

Therefore from an archetypical standpoint, women are associated with rhythm and analog modes of functioning while men are commonly associated with absence of rhythm and the digital mode of functioning. Although men and women have both characteristics and it is very dangerous to use this information to define what males and females are like or what they should be like in society, understanding these associations may help us reach a deeper understanding of language, literature, traditions, beliefs, and art created by people in various cultures. Examining and interpreting the meaning of the various traditions, literature, and art in various cultures can provide us many clues concerning how the mind works. One of the most commonly examined and widely discussed topics concerning variation in culture is the difference between Western and Eastern cultures. The next section briefly discusses the differences between Western and Eastern cultures from the perspective of anxiety, desires, and energy.

EAST VERSUS WEST

Earlier, we discussed the two ways to deal with the separation between our desires and what has, is, or might be (i.e., the cause of anxiety). One way is to steal energy. It is to control and dominate things so that our desires win over what has, is, or might happen. The other way was to open up our pores and experience unity. It is to let go of our desires when they do not match what has, is, or might happen. These are the two ways of dealing with differentiation and separation (and anxiety which is the cause of this) and can be roughly associated with the two general cultural traditions between the East and the West. Although various cultures lie on the continuum of the East-West continuum, it may be safe to say that the term "Westernization" refers to the move from the tendency to let go of our desires to a tendency to control things so that our desires win over what has, is, or might happen. Therefore, Eastern (or non-Western) cultures are identified as cultures that deal with differentiation and anxiety by letting go of desires whereas Western cultures are typically identified as cultures that deal with differentiation and anxiety by controlling things.

We can see that the majority of Eastern philosophies (though not all of them) such as Hinduism, Taoism, and Buddhism focus on letting go of our desires while the majority of the popular Western philosophies (though not all of them) such as those of Descartes, and Newton focus on prediction and control (i.e., making our desires win over what has, is, or might happen). This is also related to the idea that Eastern (or non-Western) cultures emphasize the groups one belongs to rather than the self as an individual. Focusing on the group (i.e., what is good for your group rather than yourself as an individual) requires letting go of our personal desires. On the other hand, Western cultures that emphasize the person as an individual (rather than as members of groups) provide freedom to individuals in order to realize their personal desires by controlling the environment.

Furthermore, the controlling nature of Western cultures tends to make them rely more on rigid social structure such as rules, regulations, contracts, policies, and laws, in order to maintain order in society. Thus, Western cultures tend to be more advanced with regulations, policies, laws concerning contracts, and legal practices, and emphasize these structures much more than Eastern (non-Western) cultures. For example, it is much more common to settle business or personal disputes using the legal system in the United States (a nation with a "Western" Culture) than in Japan (a nation with an "Eastern" culture).

In contrast, the tendency to let go of our desires in Eastern (non-Western) cultures has lead to the development of more subtle ways to maintain order in society. People in Eastern (non-Western) cultures tend to prefer settling business and personal disputes behind closed doors without the use of rigid structures such as the legal system, contracts, or organizational policies. Rather than settling disputes by having rigid structures (such as the legal system, signing contracts, developing organizational policies) that control the situation, they prefer developing a sense of unity among the individuals or groups involved in order to settle disputes. This requires person to person contact and accepting and respecting the other party's desires as well as letting go of one's own desires to some extent.

The tendency for Western cultures to control things (so that our desires win over what may happen) has also caused them to become more industrialized and advanced in technology in general. All of these advances enhance the survival rates of people in these cultures (since people have a *desire* to live). For example, technology facilitates the production and distribution of resources such as food, electricity, petroleum etc. In addition, medical advances allow for better treatment and protection from diseases. This tendency to control things, however, has also caused Western cultures to colonize and destroy nature as well (it makes us *desire* to control other people and land). Thus we can see that there are both positive and negative characteristics that evolve from these tendencies. In contrast, the tendency of Eastern (non-Western) cultures to let go of their desires has caused slower development in the areas of industrialization and technology in general. Because of the tendency to let go of our desires, people in these cultures do not desire things to change, thus development in trying to control things occurs at a slower pace. On the other hand, this tendency has also caused Eastern (non-Western) cultures to colonize and destroy nature less. Recent Westernization of these cultures, however, have moved them closer to the characteristics of Western cultures who traditionally have more of a tendency to control things rather than letting go of desires. On the other hand, recent developments concerning the notion of self-development in the realm of psychology, philosophy, ecology, and spirituality in the Western world has moved the West slightly closer to the traditional views of Eastern cultures. Perhaps evolution is designed to balance each other out so that when one set of cultures move in one direction, the other cultures move in the other direction. It may be useful to think about the characteristics of various cultures in the context of evolution since cultural development relates highly to the process of evolution.

EVOLUTION

Various scholars have suggested that the evolution of matter occurs from the simple to the complex[36]. Atoms organize together to form a more complex system called molecules. Molecules organize to form more complex systems like cells. Cells organize to form more complex systems like multi-cellular organisms (e.g., humans). Multi-cellular organisms like humans organize themselves to form groups of organisms like families. Families organize to form communities and communities organize to form nations etc. Such is the nature of evolution. Any system at any level during the course of evolution has two general tendencies. One tendency is self-preservation. Any system, whether it is an atom or molecule, cell, or multi-cellular organism has the tendency to preserve its own integrity. Atoms have the tendency to stay intact unless something radical happens to them. Human individuals have the tendency to stay intact unless something radical happens to them (this is the survival instinct). Nations have the tendency to preserve themselves. The other tendency that all systems of every level have is the tendency to integrate themselves into a larger whole. Any system is motivated to unite with other systems and organize into a larger whole. Atoms organize themselves to form molecules. People tend to organize themselves into communities and communities tend to organize themselves into towns. Thus with these two tendencies, systems integrate with each other to develop more and more complex systems. Although evolution has branched off in many directions and there are different systems at similar levels of organization (e.g., different species of reptiles), there are systems within more complex systems within even more complex systems. And the further we go in the evolutionary process, the more we witness the evolution of ever more complex systems[37].

These two tendencies are also related to the two modes of functioning described earlier. The digital mode of functioning corresponds to the tendency toward self-preservation. With the digital mode of functioning, we differentiate and self-preservation requires the differentiation between self and non-self. In order to have the concept of self-preservation, we also need to differentiate life from death. Furthermore, we need to identify with the category of life and try to win over death. This tendency for self-preservation also corresponds to our experiences in the middle of the horizontal axis of Figure 3 where we experience a sense of separation and perceive things as either taking or giving energy. Similarly, when we are in this digital mode of functioning, we experience things as either taking or giving energy (i.e., winning or losing). And in order to preserve ourselves, we want to take energy rather than give energy. When my tendency toward self-preservation is at work, I want my desires to be attended to. In situations like this, attending to the desires of others is not of primary concern. Thus, I am motivated to take energy rather than give. This applies to self-preservation of systems at any level, whether we are examining a molecule, an individual person, or a nation.

The analog mode of functioning corresponds to the tendency toward integration into a larger whole. In order to integrate into a larger system, any system needs to focus on how things go together. In order to integrate, we need to relate and connect with other systems and form a larger overall pattern by working together with the other systems. Individuals need to relate and connect to each other to form communities. Atoms need to relate and connect to each other to form molecules. In order to integrate, the systems involved must communicate well and develop an understanding relationship with each other. This means that all parties need to attend to each other and respond to each other's desires appropriately (i.e., give and take energy in a smooth rhythm). Thus, when all parties give and take relatively equal amounts of energy in a smooth rhythm with each other, they begin integrating and forming a larger system. This formation of the larger system is analogous to the experience of unity/togetherness, the right end of the horizontal axis in Figure 3.

Therefore, separation (giving and taking of energy) and unity/togetherness are part of the process of evolution. From this perspective, we could speculate that the various systems that exist today will eventually integrate with each other to form even larger, more encompassing systems. In order for this to occur, the systems will need to communicate well and develop an understanding relationship with each other so that we can be in sync with each other (i.e., move from the left to the right side of the horizontal axis in Figure 3). In others words, in order for us to feel more stable and experience more unity/togetherness, we as individuals or communities or nations, will need to attend to each other and respond to each other's desires appropriately (i.e., give and take energy equally in a smooth rhythm). This will enable us to form larger integrative systems with sub-systems that are respectful and attentive to each other. The less we attend to the environment (individuals, communities, nations, organisms etc.), the less stable we will be and the less unity/togetherness we will experience. The more we take from the environment without giving back (individuals, communities, nations, organisms etc.), the more the environment will take back from us and the less unity/togetherness we will experience with them (and the slower our evolutionary progress because integration is progress). Thus although the taking of energy and the tendency for self-preservation is important in life or death (of the system) circumstances (so that evolution does not go in the reverse direction from complex to simple systems)[38], the tendency to integrate and unite is an integral part of natural evolutionary development.

This idea suggests that there is a specific direction in evolution. Although at a non-conscious level, the universe is, was, and always will be in unity regardless of what we do or think, our consciousness is changing. At a conscious level, we seem to be moving from conscious separation to conscious unity bringing matter/energy together to form ever larger consciously organized wholes. Thus we are witnessing the evolution of consciousness from individual consciousness, to tribal/national consciousness, and presently we are witnessing the beginnings of to global consciousness and a tiny bit of cosmic consciousness. And as conscious beings, we can contribute to this evolution by developing our own consciousness and helping others develop this type of consciousness. This will facilitate the development of ever larger wholes. In order to develop into ever larger wholes, we must learn to respect other individuals, other tribes/nations as well as other organisms and matter/energy, just as we would like to be respected. We must learn to become less self-centered.

The formation of ever larger wholes is achieved by increasing peace and harmony among all holons at all levels of functioning. For example, world peace is a goal for many groups of individuals in the present world. Environmental harmony of our planet may be another common goal for many groups among the world. When this is achieved we will strive for greater peace with the universe outside of our planet (although this is difficult to imagine because most of us are not at that stage to think about it yet). Even though we do have cruelty, violence, wars in the present world, we notice that there is less cruelty, less violence, less warfare, less slavery, and more respect for fellow humans in general than ever before. This is due to this process of evolution. As we evolve, we become less self-centered and we become more respectful of other people, groups, organisms, and nature in general. Thus, we experience more unity and peace as we evolve and continue to evolve. Indeed, unity and peace may perhaps be the never-ending goal of our existence.

This concept of evolution is analogous to the concept of human development in many ways. Just as physical systems continuously unite to form larger wholes, our self-system continuously unites with new experiences to form ever larger self-systems. In the last section of this book, we will examine human development and the life cycle using this perspective.

Human Development

DEVELOPMENT AND ARRESTED DEVELOPMENT

This process of evolution discussed above may also be applied to the development of the mind from a psychological perspective. Our mind is an integral system that enables us to understand our experiences. Although every experience we have is somewhat new, some experiences are very similar to one's we have had before. The more similar the experience is to past ones, the less we need to change our self-system because we already have quite an adequate system to understand this new experience (Jean Piaget referred to as "assimilation"[39]). The less similar it is from our past experiences, the more we must change our self-system to understand it. When this happens, we periodically experience a state of chaos and confusion until we develop a new system that enables us to understand all of our past experiences including the new experience that caused us the confusion. This process, which Jean Piaget called "accommodation", continues on and on as we experience new things throughout our lives. Some experiences are radically different from anything we have experienced before and thus cause more chaos than others. Because we continue having new experiences throughout our lives, we experience chaos periodically, over and over again. In this way, our mind goes through a cycle of relative stability and chaos throughout our lives, evolving into an ever more complex system (i.e, self-system) every time we experience something new. This is the rhythm of stability and instability (or chaos and order). The mind keeps expanding to form systems that are more and more comprehensive enabling us to understand and adjust to an increasingly wider range of experiences.

Figure 20 is an aerial view of the ocean analogy (view from the top). The area identified as the self-system is the space taken by all of the things you feel unity with (basically what you perceive as the self). When some new experience influences us, water is poured in from outside the self. This makes the self-system break down periodically and makes us experience chaos and confusion for a while. After the self-system reorganizes itself so that the new experience is integrated into the self-system, we have a more inclusive, wider ranging self-system than before. Now we are able to understand and comfortably deal with a wider range of situations than before. In other words, we are now able to stay in unity with a wider range of things, people, and situations than we did before. The self-system is larger afterwards in Figure 20 because we are experiencing unity with a wider range of things than before.

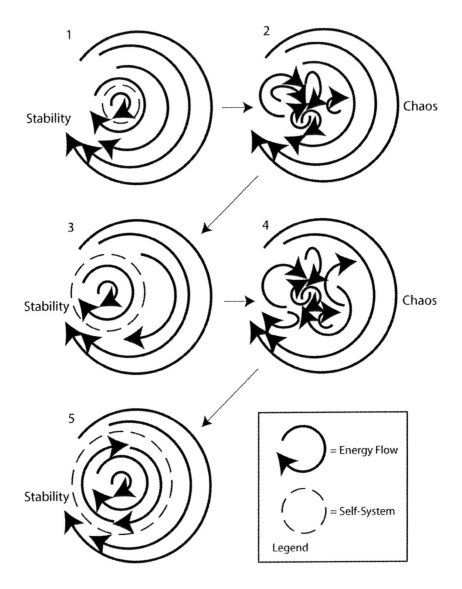

Figure 20. Development of the Self-System

When our present self-system and a new experience cannot be integrated, we experience a separation (between our present self-system and the new experience). We build a thick shell around our self-system and to shield ourselves from to new experience. This is what happens when we choose to ignore, deny, or repress a new experience and remain anxious having thick and hard shells (we fear things that we cannot understand). If we decide to face this new experience and allow it to influence us, we experience temporary confusion or chaos. This is exactly why we fear new things we do not understand. We do not like the confusion and chaos it causes in our mind. In order to enable the unification of the present system and the new experience, we must let go of our desire to preserve our self-system (i.e., self, pride) and allow our self-system to break down and integrate itself with the new experience.

Therefore, our mind is in a constant cycle of differentiation and integration as it integrates more and more new information that was initially experienced as separate and unintegratable. When experiences are different from what we are used to, we differentiate it from our self-system. If we are courageous enough, we allow it to influence us. When it influences us, we periodically experience chaos because the new experience does not make sense if we try to understand it with our existing self-system. Therefore, the self-system reorganized itself so that the all of our experiences including the new experience makes sense to us. This is what we mean by integration. Although the cycle of differentiation and integration seems like a nice rhythmic process, it is not always that consistent. New separations can occur before integration of a former experience occurs. Therefore, in many cases, a person may have many experiences that are not integrated at one time. We commonly experience multiple events in a short span of time without having the opportunity to integrate the experiences into our self-system. The more this happens, the more confused, fragmented, anxious, and unstable the person feels.

Furthermore, when a new experience is too powerfully different from anything we have experienced before, we often repress or deny the experience. In this case, the new experience is too different and causes more confusion and chaos than the mind can bear. Because it is too much for our mind, we automatically shut it out and ignore it as if it was not experienced. In other words, our system dominates over the new experience by disrespecting it or ignoring its force (i.e., not attending to its desires in human relationship terms). When this happens, our system not only ignores that particular information, but it inhibits further development in general. When we shut out a new experience, we harden our shell. The harder shell helps to protect our selves from this new threatening information only to certain extent. The problem with denial and repression (i.e., the thicker shell) is that the information does not merely disappear. It is still there and it is still influencing us (we sink deeper in the ocean and more water seeps in). In addition, as mentioned in earlier sections, we lose touch with our true inner feelings.

The more experiences we repress or deny, the thicker our shells become and the deeper we sink into the ocean (see Figure 4). The deeper we sink into the ocean, the more water and less air we have and thus the less energy we feel. When we deny or repress new experiences, we not only allow ourselves to have less energy, we also feel more desperate to retain the small amount of energy we have left. This makes us become self-protective and steal energy from the environment (i.e., close our pores and dump water on others). The less we allow new experiences to influence us, the less our system expands and the less we develop. As time goes by, we may have more and more experiences that are not integrated if we have hard shells. If we have thick hard shells, we fail to learn from those experiences because we do not let anything new inside. This is the experience of arrested development. The more emotional baggage we have, the more difficult it is to not only deal with our own baggage, but to integrate any new experience we have afterwards. Because of this, we can say that the more emotional baggage we have, the more we keep falling behind in our development. It is a negative cycle that snowballs as time goes on until we are able to integrate our painful and chaos causing experiences into a new system of understanding. When we are able to integrate the new experience in our self-system we move forward in our development. Moving forward in our development is like a small step toward transcendence. To explore how this relates to transcendence, let's concentrate on the notion of development in relation to our self-system and transcendence and examine this in further detail.

DEVELOPMENT AS MINI-TRANSCENDENCE

A new experience is always a chance to develop. When we have a new experience, we rebuild our self-system. The reason why we do this is because this enables us to rebuild our patterns that enable us to satisfy our own desires (i.e., experience energy) more effectively than before. We become more effective than before because now we know how to satisfy our desires in a wider variety of situations. Our understanding of the world includes and transcends our understanding before that experience. We know how to satisfy our desires in all of the situations we have encountered before, plus the new situation (which was the source of the new experience). This type of development leads to the development of new patterns that include and transcend the former pattern. When we develop out of certain patterns, we intuitively understand the former patterns we used to use and can relate to the people who use patterns similar to that. However, we now have different and more effective patterns. This is why individuals who have a wide variety of experiences (that they have integrated into their system) tend to be very wise and understanding of others. They understand others well because they are likely to have had similar experiences before. They know the patterns of these other people very well because they themselves used to have them and they also know how (or at least one way) to break out of (i.e., transcend) these patterns because they have done so themselves. Many times, these are the people who serve as our role models, counselors, teachers and true leaders in our lives (though not necessarily professionally).

When we are able to break out of a certain pattern, it is a process of integrating a new experience into our self-system. In a sense, we can conceptualize development as becoming less self-centered in our perceptions and learning to see things as a game from the outside. There is a difference between blindly playing a game just to win without being conscious of the patterns we are directly involved in and playing the game with a conscious understanding of the patterns we are involved in. Let us look at an example. Let us assume that I become friends with a person called Toni and he has developed a pattern of stealing energy from me using the interrogation/criticism method. I, on the other hand, have developed a pattern of stealing energy from Toni using the self-pity method. Therefore Toni and I have developed patterns of stealing energy from each other, but neither of us is aware of this. Thus, whenever Toni or I feel low in energy, we steal energy from each other. When Toni begins stealing from me, I retaliate and steal back, and then Toni retaliates and steals back etc. When I begin stealing from Toni, Toni retaliates and steals from me, and then I retaliate and steal back from Toni, etc. The cycle can go on and on regardless of who started it (even though that is what we tend to focus on). We are constantly in a battle trying to steal energy from each other. Because neither of us is aware of this, this pattern is repeated many times every day. However, even though I am not aware of what the exact problem is, I notice that I feel uncomfortable being with Toni. This new pattern that I developed with Toni is a new experience for me and I have not yet integrated it into my self-system.

However, if I talk to an insightful therapist or gain insight from contemplating about my new situation for a while, I may be able to expand my perceptions from a self-centered one of just trying to maintain my own energy to a less self-centered perception of finding a way to enable both of us to maintain our energy. In order to expand my perceptions, I may develop a conscious awareness of this pattern of stealing energy from each other. Once I become aware of this pattern, I can perceive this pattern that I have with Toni as a type of game. It can be seen as a game just like chess or checkers. Only in this game, we take turns stealing energy from each other and the object of the game is to steal the most energy. Now that I see this as a game, I can consciously change the game. I can change the game so that the object of the game is no longer taking as much energy as you can from the other person but rather, finding a way for both of us to maintain our energy. Because I see this from a new and less self-centered perspective (now I understand and care that Toni feels depleted when I do certain things), I now have the choice of either continue playing the game with the same rules (i.e., stealing energy from Toni the way I usually do) or to change the game. Before I develop that awareness, I have no choice. I respond automatically without being conscious of what is happening. I am just playing the game assuming that the rules are unchangeable. Now that I have the choice, however, I can see this as a game we are playing and I have the freedom to play the game or change the game into something else. I can think, "Perhaps I can change the game so that the goal is not stealing energy but to find a way to experience unity with each other." This is the difference between being in a stage of development where I am not aware of the patterns I am immersed in and being in the next stage where I am aware of the pattern and have the choice to do something to change the pattern.

Sometimes, however, we feel we are aware of a pattern that we do not like but cannot figure out how to change the pattern. When we feel this way, there are two possibilities. One is that we are involved in a pattern that is so powerful that changing it requires a serious threat to our life. The other and more likely possibility is that we are not understanding the true nature of the pattern. In many cases, we may feel like we understand the pattern but are actually contributing to the maintenance (and sometimes exacerbation) of the pattern without being aware of it.

For example, I may realize that Toni has a pattern of stealing energy from me using the interrogation/criticism method and I even realize that I steal energy from Toni using the self-pity method. I feel like I understand the pattern and try to stop this pattern, I stop using the self-pity method on Toni. Even when I stop using the self-pity method on Toni, I find that Toni still keeps stealing energy from me using the interrogation/criticism method as much as he did before. I may feel disappointed because I thought I understood the pattern and I tried to change it but it did not work. I feel like even though I know what the pattern is, I cannot do anything about it. This is where we usually blame something else such as the other person, the theory, or anything else that may be convenient and give up. However, even though I may not be aware of this, an insightful therapist may point out that I have another method of stealing energy that I am using on Toni that I have either replaced or have always had in combination with the self-pity method. Therefore, even though I have stopped using the self-pity method on Toni, I may now be stealing energy from Toni by using the aloofness method and this may be motivating Toni to steal as much energy from me as he used to. Unless we are aware of this other method, we may feel like there is nothing we can do even though we understand our patterns (even though we really do not). An important thing to remember is that it always takes all of the individuals in a pattern to both create and sustain a pattern. We are always contributors in the patterns we are involved with.

If we do become aware of these patterns and are able to change our patterns into something more peaceful and less selfish, we can say that we have developed a new pattern and a new system of understanding. This is the beauty of true development. It allows you to notice the game you are playing and allows you to change the game into something less selfish than before. When we are able to change a game into something less selfish that makes more people and things comfortable than before, we have truly integrated our experience into our self-system. In general, the more we develop, the more our game is geared toward having a larger number of people and things feeling happy, respected, and energized. This is because the more we develop the more we are able to see things from the perspective of a wider variety of people (and things). The more we are able to see things from other people's perspectives, the more we are able to match our desires with those of other people (and therefore experience more unity with them).

When we change and develop, we form a system of understanding that includes and transcends the pattern and system of understanding we had before the change. We can say that it includes and transcends our former pattern/system because we see things from a wider or deeper perspective and thus the pattern we subconsciously engaged in before, now seems like a game. Our self-system is now able to handle a wider variety of situations more comfortably than before. In the example with my relationship with Toni, I now can interact with Toni without stealing energy from each other even though I was not able to before. At the same time, this enabled me to comfortably maintain the energy levels of a larger number (i.e., from 1 to 2 in this example) of people than before. The more we develop, the more we are able to handle a wider variety of situations comfortably and the more we learn to peacefully co-exist with a wider range of people and things in our environment. Thus, every time we develop, we have a slight experience of transcendence. Just like physical holons uniting and transcending themselves to form larger wholes (e.g., atoms to molecules), every time we develop, we transcend our patterns and form a larger (more widely encompassing) self-system.

In order to develop and transcend our present self-system, we need to be somewhat critical of our own self-system to some extent. It is important to be aware that our self-systems are never complete and that development is a never-ending process. This helps us maintain an open mind so that we can allow things to influence us and thus continue learning and developing. This is the reason why many people consider critical thinking to be an important element in our developmental process.

CRITICAL THINKING AND DEVELOPMENT

Although critical thinking is commonly regarded as an important skill, there is good critical thinking, which promotes development and there is bad critical thinking, which often impedes development. Although development always involves the breaking down of and restructuring of all of the self-systems involved in the larger context, some involve the breaking down of one's own self-system more than the breaking down of the self-systems of the environment (i.e., other people & things), while others involve the breaking down of self-systems in the environment more than the breaking down of one's own self-system.

The type of critical thinking that promotes development is thinking that involves the breaking down of and reorganization of one's own self-system rather than the breaking down of the self-systems of the people and things in the environment. It involves a consideration of a wider variety of perspectives and information than before. This type of thinking comes from open-mindedness rather than closed mindedness. This type of thinking often leads to transcending one's own or one's group's understanding of something and developing the ability to see things from a wider variety of perspectives. It is the act of opening our pores and allowing things to influence us in order to transcend our present understanding of things.

In contrast, the type of critical thinking that impedes development is thinking that involves the breaking down of the self-systems in the environment (i.e., other people & things) rather than the breaking down of one's own self-system. It is often identified as criticism for the sake of putting things down and making oneself look superior. This type of critical thinking comes from closed-mindedness rather than open-mindedness. This is criticism due to the inability to accept new perspectives, possibilities, and information because of fear of breaking down our own self-system that we are comfortable using or just plain laziness to reorganize our own self-system. It forces our environment to adjust to our own self-system more than ourselves adjusting to the self-system of the environment. It is the act of closing our pores and stealing energy from the environment. When we use the interpersonal behavior pattern of criticism / interrogation, this is precisely what we are doing.

This is the reason why people say, "do not tell others what to do, lead by example." When we do not like something, changing ourselves to adjust to the situation is true development. Changing the environment to make it adjust to us comes from defensiveness and laziness (even though we do this all of the time). It is a sign that we are refusing to change and refusing to adjust our self-system (i.e., you are refusing to develop). If we truly want to be happy, we need to constantly adapt to the environment and instead of stealing energy from the environment. This involves being critical of one's own self-system rather than being critical of the self-systems of others.

Although development is a life-long continuous process, some stages of life are more harmonious and less chaotic than others. For instance, adolescence is commonly considered to be a more chaotic and less harmonious stage than late life. Why does this happen? The next section discusses this process from a big picture perspective concerning the life cycle.

THE CYCLE OF HUMAN LIFE

In the very beginning of our lives, everything is experienced as one blob of experience. As Martin S. Banks suggests in his research with infants, even our visual perceptions are a blob of experience[40]. This is the stage in life where we experience something close to complete unity. Because of this relative unity, infants at this stage tend to experience most things in relatively analog fashion. We are just enjoying the continuity and flow of our experiences. This is the experience of innocence. We do not differentiate this experience from that experience. We cannot tell the difference between one and two. We have not separated things in our mind yet. This unity experienced in the earlier part of life is considered to be subconscious. As we develop early in life we develop consciousness and with consciousness comes the differentiation of our experiences. I am different from you. I have desires that are separate from mommy's desires (i.e., what has, is, or might happen). This is primarily what happens when we develop in the early parts of life. We primarily differentiate our experiences during this time and we divide the world into our desires and all of the things that might happen, has happened, or is happening. In addition, we try to figure out ways to control our surroundings so that our desires win over what has, is, or might happen. This is commonly perceived as cognitive development or the development of intelligence.

As we differentiate our experiences more and more, this continuity and flow of our experience becomes more and more like a rhythm, until many of our experiences become almost completely digitized and separated. The more our experiences are digitized, the more potential there is for conflict. We see things as this way or that way, you or me, us or them, right or wrong, good or bad. When this happens we identify with one side of the conflict (i.e., my desires) and try to dominate the other side (i.e., what has, is, or might happen). To do this, we steal energy from people and things. The more digitized our experience, the more we are immersed in the battle of trying to win over the other side by breaking down, destroying, denying, or repressing the other side. This is how many of our conflicts become serious battles. When we begin experiencing things in this way, it is no longer a game of give and take. It is take and take and refuse to lose (i.e., give). It is no longer something to enjoy. We are serious and our priority is to win. We want to win in business, politics, sports, arguments, or just family and work relationships. This is what happens when we gradually grow out of our innocence and become "adults". We create boundaries, develop hard shells to protect ourselves, become competitive, manipulative and controlling because we want to win and dominate. We want things to go our way (i.e., desires) and not any other way.

Furthermore, as we learn to differentiate many things, we begin to realize that our desire is one little thing among many many many possible things in the world and we do not yet realize how this separation between my desires and what has, is, or might happen is the cause of conflict. The more we differentiate these things, the more we battle to make our desires win over what is, what has, or what might happen. The more battles we have, the more potential there is to lose a higher number of battles. The more battles we lose, the more powerless, small, inferior, and weak (i.e., anxiety) we feel. In order to feel less powerless, we use defenses and try to control these things (i.e., steal energy) using our analytical and logical abilities and technological tools (because this makes us feel stronger and better). This is the move from unity/togetherness to instability and chaos. This experience corresponds to the commonly discussed literary concepts such as "Exile from Eden", "Paradise lost", the "loss of innocence", and relates to everyday expressions as "growing up fast", and "welcome to the world (as sarcasm)".

During this early period of our lives, there is more differentiation and less integration throughout our process of development. Because of this, our understanding of the world becomes more and more differentiated and fragmented as we develop during the early periods of our lives. The more desires we have, the more potential there is for unfulfilled desires. The more desires we have, the more things (what has, is, or might happen) we must compete against. The more things we must compete against, the more alienated we feel. Thus, the period between adolescence and middle age is often a period of alienation and dealing with alienation. Because this is the period of alienation, this period is perhaps the most active, productive, busy (because we are trying to control things so that our desires come true), but also tumultuous, confusing, and chaotic period in our lives. During this period we struggle to find our own identity, we struggle to develop ways to make a living, we struggle to protect and take care of our children. We struggle to gain respect, attention, and control both socially and physically. Furthermore, the process of reproduction, which commonly occurs in this period, may be a product of this experience of alienation. It may be that we reproduce to make more of us. This is because making more of us makes us feel less alienated, and it also makes us feel more powerful and in control.

In the very early stages when we are infants, very little is differentiated and thus we experience very little alienation. As we grow older, we differentiate much more than we are able to integrate. This causes us to feel more and more differentiated as well as more and more alienated. As we reach a certain point in our lives (typically considered midlife), the differentiations slow down and integration begins to catch up. In these latter parts of life, we begin to spend more energy integrating many of our experiences into our system of understanding and less energy differentiating our experiences. In other words, we begin letting go of our desires more and more and learn to accept our experiences as they come. We begin surfing on the waves (i.e., rhythm of life) rather than fighting them. Perhaps this is why psychologists such as Carl Jung state that "true development" occurs primarily in the latter parts of life[41].

If we use the ocean analogy, we learn to ride the waves as the water ebbs and flows through and under our bodies in the latter parts of life. This enables us to experience more and more unity/togetherness. Somewhere in mid-life we peak in our digital mode of functioning. This peak occurs at different times for different individuals. Some may peak at 30 years of age. Others may peak at 75 years of age. After we peak, we gradually develop out of this digital mode of thought and we begin letting our desires go and trusting life and uniting with all of the things we are fighting against. When this happens, we stop playing the game primarily to win. Rather, we begin playing the game more for the sake of *playing* the game (i.e., enjoying the process). We do it for the sake of interacting with people/things and maintaining and developing relationships, and experiencing unity/togetherness with other people and things. During this phase, we begin to experience things more and more in the analog mode. Our lives are experienced as having more continuity and flow and we begin experiencing more of a sense of unity and togetherness with everything and everyone else. This process is commonly conceptualized as the development of wisdom.

People who cannot make the switch from primarily differentiating to primarily integrating typically experience a mid-life crisis. A mid-life crisis occurs when we primarily still differentiate even though society expects us to begin integrating more due to how old we look. Eventually many of those people who experience a mid-life crisis make the switch into the mode of primarily using integration and mature like the rest of the people their age. Most of us, however, do not have a mid-life crisis and make the transition into the second half of life quite smoothly.

In sum, we begin with unity/togetherness and move gradually towards more and more differentiation and separation during the middle of our lives. After this, we focus more on integrating what we have differentiated and gradually move back towards unity/togetherness. This is the cycle of life. Let us look at it from the perspective of how the self-system works. In the earlier part of life where differentiation occurs more rapidly than integration, there are many things in our conscious awareness that are not integrated in our self-system. In this earlier part of life, we feel comfortable as long as we are functioning within our self-system but our self-system is not well developed yet. In other words, there are many things in our conscious awareness that has not been integrated into the self-system. Thus we spend much of our time trying to maintain our energy primarily by taking large amounts of energy from the things that are not yet integrated into our self-system (i.e., controlling things). In the latter part of life, where integration occurs more rapidly than differentiation, many things in our conscious awareness become integrated into our self-system. If we look at Figure 20, we notice that the more we develop, the more inclusive and wider ranging our self-system becomes. This makes it easier for us to stay within our self-system and maintain our energy primarily by experiencing unity (because we are in unity with all of the things in our self-system)[42].

In sum, we move from non-conscious unity to conscious differentiation to conscious unity. This implies that the unity experienced before things are differentiated early in life is different from the unity experienced after the differentiation later in life. We may argue that the unity experienced in the first part of life is unity without conscious awareness whereas unity experienced in the latter part of life is a conscious experience of unity since we have consciously integrated what we have differentiated at this point. This may be true because conscious unity must involve a boundary while unconscious unity does not. Even if we consciously understand that everything is one, there must be something outside of everything to consciously conceptualize "everything". In other words, because there is no stage in life where a person has integrated every single thing that can possibly be differentiated, we always have a relatively closed system that has integrated some things but not everything. On the other hand, non-conscious unity, the completely complete unity experienced before and after existence is the same because complete unity, whether it is before or after differentiation, requires the complete absence of consciousness.

Some may argue that this view makes our life seem pointless because we just come back to the same state as we started. According to this view, the purpose is in the cycle. There is no end point required. There is no change that is required to make things meaningful from this perspective. The earth does not revolve around the sun with a specific goal in mind. It just does so. The whole point is that change is a natural part of a larger cycle and in the end, we come back to where we started. The reason why we do not notice this in most cases is that we fail to see the larger cycle. Sometimes the cycle is so large (e.g., the cycle lasting from the beginning to the end of the universe), that we do not realize that things will eventually return to where we were before. This concept of cycles and rhythms can only be understood with the analog mode of functioning. The analog mode is very different from the digital mode in that it requires no end point and events are perceived more as infinite, rhythmic, and perhaps circular rather than linear (everything causing everything else rather than one thing causing the other). In the analog mode of functioning, the meaning is in the rhythm or in the process. In the linear mode of functioning, the meaning is in the end goal (and the difference between the beginning and the end).

When we begin to see the meaning in the cycle rather than in the goal, the life cycle is a beautiful thing to behold. Every stage in life has its beauty and significance and every stage is beautiful because we see it in relation to the other stages. However, we have the general tendency to be attracted to youth and fear old age. This tendency is especially pronounced in the Western world. Why does this happen? Is it merely because we are afraid of death or is there more to this story? Let's examine this in the next section.

THE BEAUTY OF YOUTH AND OLD AGE

In the Western world, we commonly perceive youth as activeness, physical power, dominance, and stamina. We also associate it with attractiveness and attracting attention from people in general. All of these concepts relates to the concept of control. We have the tendency to perceive old age as the opposite of this. We perceive it as becoming weak, losing physical control (body movements and health in general). We have the tendency to view things on the vertical axis in Figure 3. We associate youth with dominance and old age with submissiveness and passivity. However, this is only half or perhaps even less than half of he whole picture.

Because things in radical rhythms of giving and taking tend to attract our attention, we notice these things more. Not only do we notice it more but we identify with the person/object that is taking energy because it attracts lots of attention and we are amazed at the power that the person or object has. We commonly identify with winners and we are attracted to influential people and powerful objects.

When we mature and grow wiser, we begin to notice that the person/object is taking at the cost of another person/object losing energy. We notice that there are no winners if there are no losers. We notice that no one can be influential if there are no people to influence. This is the beauty of old age. We notice the bigger picture more and more and realize that the goal of life is not to become powerful and overpower other people/things (i.e., take energy from other people/things) but to enjoy a harmonious relationship with other things and people.

When we age, we don't simply move from submissiveness (in infancy) to dominance and back to submissiveness (or passivity), although this is what we commonly assume (due to the obvious gain and subsequent loss of physical powers). We are actually moving from the right to the middle and then back to the right rather than the bottom to top and then top to the bottom. We go from stable to unstable and then unstable to stable, from harmony to chaos and chaos to harmony. The move from harmony to chaos is the process of losing one's innocence. The move from chaos back to harmony is the development of wisdom. Only the people who do not see aging as moving back from the middle to the right find the process of aging torturous. They keep differentiating more than integrating and thus do not find their way back home. When this happens, aging is merely perceived as a process of physical and social deterioration, which is associated with loss of both physical and social power. As mentioned earlier, this is the experience of a mid-life crisis. If we realize that true aging is a maturation process that largely involves the integration of experiences (characterized by the movement from unstable to stable, from chaos to harmony), aging can be a beautiful thing. Late life can be seen and should be regarded as a time of harmony, wisdom, and balance.

The problem is that because the loss of physical vigor and health during the aging process is highly noticeable, we fail to see anything else. We think that it is whole story about aging. It is however, less than half of the story. Life is a constant maturation process. Although the maturation may be both physical and psychological in the early parts of life, it is largely psychological in the latter parts of life. Although perhaps this may be perceived as a rationalization made by aging individuals, it seems that the psychological maturation that takes place in this part of life may be the most important factor related to the actual quality of our lives. Physical maturation only takes place in the first twenty or so years in our life and for most of us fortunate individuals who are able to live for many years beyond our forty's, life after this period of physical maturation is much longer. And learning to appreciate and enjoy that part of life may be the essence of a truly fulfilling and wonderful life. In fact I think I am writing this book partly because I hope that it may be of help to some people to do exactly that. I hope we can all appreciate and enjoy not only the beauty of youth but also the beauty of life after physical maturation is complete.

I thank you very much for hearing what I have to say until this point. I think I have said enough for now and feel that it is time for me to put my pen to rest. The last section is a conclusion highlighting some of the central points made throughout this book that may be helpful to remind ourselves of in our everyday lives.

Conclusion:
Putting it all together

Whew! Many things have been said and it is difficult to figure out a reasonable way to put it all together. In order to conclude, I think I will just note what I think is important to remember in our everyday lives in point format. Some of these things overlap with others, but it may be useful to highlight them as separate points.

1. There is a proverb of the Arapaho North American native tribe that translates, "When we show our respect for other living things, they respond with respect for us." Perhaps this proverb sums up a large portion of this book. Life is a constant rhythm of giving and receiving of energy. Although we have the tendency to focus primarily on the receiving and forget about the giving part, the balance between giving and receiving is what really makes us happy.

2. Boundaries are merely a product of the mind. We are all connected. Everything is connected with everything. The idea that we are all separate entities is a wonderful illusion of the mind. Although this illusion is useful to some extent, it is perhaps even more useful to remember that it is an illusion.

3. We only feel bad (i.e., anxiety) when we have desires. When we are feeling bad, it is useful to think, "What is my desire at the root of my negative experience (i.e., feeling bad)" and then let go of that desire. If we can let go of that desire, it will free us from the anxiety (i.e., feeling bad).

4. If your desire is exciting you to do something, enjoy it after you have made sure that you are not stealing energy. If your desire is

causing you to be anxious, learn to change it into excitement (focus on your desire coming true rather than the possible negative outcome). For example, if you are anxious that you might lose your next chess game, focus on that fact that you might win. This will change your anxiety into excitement.

5. If you cannot change your anxiety into excitement, let go of the desire and form a new one. If your desire did not realize, let go of the desire and form a new one that is realizable from now on. For example, if you were not able to enter law school this year, let go of your desire that you wanted to get in this year. Form a new one like "I desire to enter law school in the next two years." If you are anxious because your desire seems highly unlikely, change it to something that is more likely. For instance, if you cannot stop smoking tomorrow, try to smoke a certain number of cigarettes less than usual tomorrow.

6. Desire is sometimes helpful in that it motivates us and excites us to do constructive things but it is important to remember that trying to realize our desires is just a game we are playing. As long as we are aware that everything is a game, we can enjoy the process remain flexible in our thinking. For example, if our desires do not realize or are in danger of not realizing, we do not panic if we understand that it is only a game. We can let go of the desires or change the game and form a new desire as long as we know that we are just playing a game with ourselves.

7. Realizing desires (i.e., taking energy) only makes you happy temporarily. It is like the joy of winning a game. Once we have won, we look for another game to play and try to realize our desires again. It is a never-ending process. Real happiness comes from understanding this as a game and knowing when and how to play the game and when to let go of our desires and stop playing the game.

8. As the proverb of the Cheyenne Native Tribe translates, "When you lose the rhythm of the drumbeat of God, you are lost from the peace and rhythm of life". Nature is rhythm. Life is rhythm. Learning to appreciate and respect the rhythm is learning to live a peaceful life. We must always remember to appreciate the process rather than the end goal.

9. Appreciation and gratefulness make not only others feel appreciated and respected but also makes our selves happy. Appreciation and gratefulness makes us happy because it compares the negative "what has or might happens" with "what is happening" and we identify our desires with "what is happening". For example, I may appreciate having something to eat because I compare it to having nothing to eat. This makes me happy and it may also make the people who worked hard so that I have something to eat (i.e., farmers, people who transport and sell the food, the people that cook the food) feel appreciated, recognized and respected.

10. Forgiveness sets other people free. But more importantly, it sets our selves free. When we forgive, we let go of our own desires and are able to accept what really happened. Thus by forgiving, we free ourselves from our own internal conflict.

11. As the people of the Iroquois native tribe say, "The greatest strength is gentleness." Real mental toughness is not the ability to overpower and dominate but the ability to remain in unity with the environment regardless of what happens (even if things do not go your way, even if others steal energy from you). In terms of the ocean analogy, this means keeping your shell soft and your pores open even when you feel like you are losing air. All people who are well respected have this common ability. They can remain calm, gentle, and graceful (i.e., remain in unity) and perform well without becoming defensive even when the going gets tough.

12. When we truly love and care for someone, we are willing to change ourselves for that person. When we don't truly love and care for someone, we are not willing to change for that person. Instead, we want to stay the way we are and change that person into what we want them to be like. In other words, sincerity and not necessarily honesty, is what we truly need in relationships. If people really care about each other, their desires will naturally align themselves with each other. If they do not align themselves, try to remain respectful of the other person's (people's) desires and be patient. They may eventually align themselves if we take our time.

13. Don't break anything you are not willing to fix. Sometimes we do break down people's self-system by taking energy from them in order to set boundaries or in order to help them grow. However, it is only fair to do so if you are truly prepared to be there for them afterwards and help them rebuild their self-system again.

14. Although we are tempted to steal energy from those we have power over, stealing energy is never the ultimate solution. As the proverb of the Seneca native tribe says, "He who has great power should use it lightly." Unity is the key. In order to keep experiencing high levels of unity, try to let go of your own desires and respect and attend to the desires of everyone and everything around you as much as you can.

15. All behavior is the result of anxiety (including excitement). The self-system, which directs our behaviors, is also created as a result of anxiety. We only develop a self-system because we want to maintain our energy level and we want to maintain our energy level because we want to avoid more anxiety. Any form of self-expression is the result of anxiety, a dissatisfaction of the present state. In the same way, my writing this book is a result of my wanting to influence the world (i.e., controlling things so that my desires come true. This comes from a separation of wanting to be

understood (i.e., my desire) and the possibility of feeling power-less, alienated, and not being understood in this world (i.e., what might happen). It is probably safe to assume that I want to be understood because I feel anxiety (i.e., I desire more energy and I am not transcendent). Of course, wanting some extra income from selling this book is also caused by my anxiety as well.

16. The differences between all opposing concepts are a matter of degree. Thus the differences between giving and taking (or receiving), unity and separation, opening and closing pores, soft and hard shells, digital and analog functioning, integration and differentiation, are all a matter of degree. Moreover, the difference between things inside and outside the self-system is a matter of degree. The self-system is multi-layered and things can be relatively inside or relatively outside the self-system compared to other things. The further inside we can stay, the more at home (i.e., comfortable) we feel. This goes hand in hand with the fact that we can experience relatively more or relatively less unity with other people and things (see Figure 21).

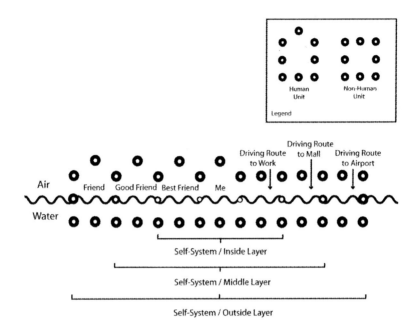

Figure 21. The Multi-layered Self-System

17. Patience and hope are wonderful virtues. We must be patient to allow people to grow at their own pace and in their own way. We must be patient to allow time for scars to heal (shells to soften). And we must have hope and not give up on our selves and others. Although we may not all be ready for a certain step in development at the same time, people do grow and people do learn when they are ready.

18. Evolutionary, personal, and social development is ongoing and is a never ending process that involves developing ever larger and more encompassing holons through mutual respect and attention. Let us look at ourselves more as participants in this process rather than controllers of this process. Before trying to make others become attentive and respectful toward others or toward ourselves, let us begin by being attentive and respectful of others ourselves. As the

people of the Sioux native tribe say, "Do not point out the way, but lead the way."

I truly thank you with all of my heart for reading this book. It is a true privilege and honor to know that some people have allowed my everyday contemplations into their lives. I sincerely hope that this journey through my ramblings has been enjoyable and interesting to you. I wish you all the luck and love in the world for the development of your own self-systems and would be delighted if anything in this book has helped in that process. I certainly feel truly blessed to have the opportunity to write this book. I have enjoyed the process of learning and thinking about these things and writing this book immensely. As I look to the future, I look forward to learning about your developments (through readings, meetings, discussions, etc.), and hope they contribute to my own development of my self-system as well.

Sincerely, Toru Sato

Endnotes

1. Sometimes we think of these "desires" as "needs" because we think they are not just things we desire, but things that are absolutely necessary. Indeed, some of these desires are absolutely necessary for physical survival. However, it is our desire for survival that makes these things necessary and thus we will use the term "desires" instead of "needs".

2. James Redfield, The Celestine Prophecy. (New York: Warner, 1993).

3. e.g., Eric Berne, Games People Play. (New York: Random House, 1964).

   Daniel Goleman, Vital Lies, Simple Truths. (New York: Simon and Schuster, 1985).

   Phillip McGraw, Life Strategies: Doing What Works, Doing What Matters. (New York: Hyperion, 1999).

   James Redfield, The Celestine Prophecy. (New York: Warner, 1993).

4. Erving Goffman, Frame Analysis. (Cambridge: Harvard University Press, 1974).

   Roger Schank & Robert Abelson, Scripts, plans, goals and understanding: An inquiry into human knowledge structures. (Hillsdale, NJ: Lawrence Erlbaum and Associates, 1977).

5. e.g., Pia Mellody, Facing Codependence: What it is, Where it comes from, How it Sabotages our Lives. (San Francisco, CA: Harper San Francisco, 1989).

Charles L. Whitfield, Codependence: Healing the Human Condition: The New Paradigm for helping Professionals and People in Recovery. (Deerfield Beach, FL: Health Communications, 1991).

6.   John Gottman, Why Marriages Succeed or Fail: And How You Can Make Yours Last. (New York: Fireside, 1995).

7.   Daniel Goleman, Emotional Intelligence: Why It Can Matter More Than IQ for Character, Health and Lifelong Achievement. (New York: Bantam Books, 1995).

8.   Daniel Goleman, Emotional Intelligence: Why It Can Matter More Than IQ for Character, Health and Lifelong Achievement. (New York: Bantam Books, 1995).

9.   Anna Freud, The Ego and the Mechanisms of Defense. (New York: International Universities Press, 1946).

Alfred Adler, Understanding Human Nature. (New York: Fawcett Books, 1981).

10. I use this analogy of the connectedness of energy because it facilitates our understanding of the connectedness of all things. This analogy, however, should not be taken literally since the there is also a connection between energy and non-energy, or matter and absence of matter.

11. Alan Watts, The Book: On the taboo against knowing who you are. (New York: Vintage Books, 1966).

Ken Wilber, No Boundary. (Boston: Shambhala, 1979).

12. e.g., Muzafer Sherif, In Common Predicament: Social Psychology of Intergroup Conflict and Cooperation. (Boston: Houghton Mifflin, 1966).

Samuel L. Gaertner, Jeffrey Mann, Audrey Murrell, & John F. Dovidio, Reducing Intergroup Bias: The benefits of recategorization.

(The Journal of Personality and Social Psychology, v. 57, pp. 239-249, 1989).

13. Having a concept of complete transcendence or complete nothingness is contradictory to the purpose of transcendence since the concept distinguishes it from non-transcendence or non-nothingness. The concept itself forms another boundary even though the purpose of this is to dissolve all boundaries.

14. Medard Boss, Existential Foundations of Medicine and Psychology. (Northvale, New Jersey: Jason Aronson, 1983).

15. Arthur Koestler, The Act of Creation. (New York: Dell, 1964).

16. Donald Snygg & Arthur Combs, Individual Behavior: A Perceptual Approach to Behavior. (New York: Harper Bros., 1959).

17. e.g., Fritjof Capra, The Web of Life: A New Understanding of Living Systems (New York: Doubleday, 1997).

    William James, The Principles of Psychology. (New York: Dover; originally published 1910).

    Ken Wilber, No Boundary. (Boston: Shambhala, 1979).

18. Jean Piaget, To Understand Is To Invent. (New York: The Viking Press, 1972).

19. Jean Piaget, To Understand Is To Invent. (New York: The Viking Press, 1972).

20. Abraham Maslow, Religions, Values and Peak Experiences. (New York: Viking Press, 1994).

21. Mihalyi Csikszentmihalyi, Flow: The Psychology of Optimal Experience. (New York: HarperCollins, 1991).

22. Carl Rogers, Client-Centered Therapy. (Boston: Houghton Mifflin, 1951).

Sigmund Freud (James Strachey, Ed.), The Standard Edition of the Complete Psychological Works of Sigmund Freud: 24 volume set. (New York: W. W. Norton, 2000).

23. Donald Snygg & Arthur Combs, Individual Behavior: A Perceptual Approach to Behavior. (New York: Harper Bros., 1959).

24. Alfred Adler, Understanding Human Nature. (New York: Fawcett Books, 1981).

25. Eric Berne, Games People Play. (New York: Random House, 1964).

26. Carl Rogers, On becoming a person: A therapist's view of psychotherapy (Boston: Houghton Mifflin, 1961).

27. Alan Watts, The Book: On the taboo against knowing who you are. (New York: Vintage Books, 1966).

Ken Wilber, No Boundary. (Boston: Shambhala, 1979).

28. e.g., Anne Katherine, Boundaries: Where You End and I Begin. (New York: Fireside, 1993).

Salvatore Minuchin, Families and Family Therapy. (Cambridge, MA: Harvard University Press).

Charles L. Whitfield, Boundaries and Relationships: Knowing, Protecting, and Enjoying the Self. (Deerfield Beach, FL: Health Communications, 1993).

29. e.g., Irving Janis, Groupthink, 2nd ed. (Boston, MA: Houghton Mifflin)

Salvatore Minuchin, Families and Family Therapy. (Cambridge, MA: Harvard University Press).

David Reiss, The Family's Construction of Reality. (Cambridge, MA: Harvard University Press, 1981).

30. It is important to note that the person who is dangerous is not necessarily the person being forced to change all of the time (although that may be the most helpful thing to do). For example, if an abusive husband is beyond the realm of our influence, the abused wife who is not willing to leave her abusive husband may be the one we may try to change in a forceful way so that she leaves him (for her safety).

31. Carl Rogers, The necessary and sufficient conditions of therapeutic personality change. (Journal of Consulting Psychology, vol. 21, pp. 95-103, 1957).

32. Erich Fromm, Escape from Freedom. (New York: Henry Holt, 1995).

33. e.g., Aaron Beck, Cognitive Therapy and the Emotional Disorders. (New York: International Universities Press, 1976).

    Albert Ellis, Reason and Emotion in Psychotherapy (2nd ed.). (Saecaucus, NJ: Lyle Stuart, 1977).

34. Stanley Schachter & Jerome Singer, Cognitive, social and psychological determinants of emotional state. (Psychological Review, v. 69, pp. 379-399, 1962).

35. The difference is caused by the differing perspectives. When we subjectively view the relationship as something we are directly involved in, we notice that we are merely in a rhythm of giving and taking. If, however, we view the relationship objectively from a third person perspective, it looks like a rhythm changing between smoothness and roughness. This is because we have the general tendency to pay more attention to things interacting in a rough manner than things interacting in a smooth manner. This also applies to the concept of having a rhythm of opening and closing our pores. The rhythm of opening and closing our pores corresponds to the rhythm between smoothness and roughness. We pay attention only when the pores are closed (which leads to roughness).

36. e.g., Fritjof Capra, The Web of Life: A New Understanding of Living Systems. (New York: Doubleday, 1997).

Arthur Koestler, The Act of Creation. (New York: Dell, 1964).

Ken Wilber, Sex, Ecology, Spirituality: The Spirit of Evolution. (Boston: Shambhala, 1995).

37. For details concerning this view of evolution, please refer to; Arthur Koestler, The Act of Creation. (New York: Dell, 1964), & Ken Wilber, Sex, Ecology, Spirituality: The Spirit of Evolution. (Boston: Shambhala, 1995).

38. We know that systems do break down from complex to simple (e.g., our bodies decompose after we die) but as long as there is more integration than disintegration at any system level as a whole, evolution continues moving forward.

39. Jean Piaget, To Understand Is To Invent. (New York: The Viking Press, 1972).

40. Martin S. Banks, The development of visual accommodation during early infancy. (Child Development, v. 51, pp. 646-666, 1980). This work suggests that things look like a borderless blob in early infancy. It suggests that we develop the ability to see boundaries as we grow.

41. Carl Jung, The Development of Personality (Collected Works of C.G. Jung Vol.17). (Princeton, New Jersey: Princeton University Press, 1981).

42. Although we are differentiating the things inside the self-system from the things outside of the self-system for the sake of simplicity, it is not a fixed, static boundary. Not only do the boundaries move inwards or outwards from time to time, there are also various layers of boundaries in the self-system. Certain things may be considered to be inside the self-system relative to some things but

outside the self-system relative to other things. For example, even though I may perceive my uncle to be inside the self-system relative to a complete stranger, I perceive my uncle to be outside of my self-system relative to my children. In the same way, my driving route to the nearest shopping mall may be perceived as inside the self-system relative to a less familiar driving route to a town 80 miles away even though I perceive my driving route to the same shopping mall to be outside of my self-system relative to my every day driving route to work.

0-595-26222-8